Lydia Pinkham

Lydia Pinkham

The Face That
Launched a Thousand Ads

Sammy R. Danna

ROWMAN & LITTLEFIELD
Lanham • Boulder • New York • London

Published by Rowman & Littlefield
A wholly owned subsidiary of The Rowman & Littlefield Publishing Group, Inc.
4501 Forbes Boulevard, Suite 200, Lanham, Maryland 20706
www.rowman.com

Unit A, Whitacre Mews, 26-34 Stannary Street, London SE11 4AB

British Library Cataloguing in Publication Information Available

Library of Congress Cataloging-in-Publication Data

Danna, Sammy R. (Sammy Richard), 1934-
  Lydia Pinkham : the face that launched a thousand ads / Sammy R. Danna.
     pages   cm
  Includes bibliographical references and index.
  ISBN 978-0-8108-8908-8 (cloth : alk. paper) — ISBN 978-0-8108-8909-5 (ebook)
  1. Pinkham, Lydia Estes, 1819-1883. 2. Women in medicine—United States—Biography.
  3. Patent medicines—United States—History—19th century. 4. Advertising--Medicine. I.
Title.
  RM671.A1D25 2014
  610.82—dc23
                                                                2013026290

♾™ The paper used in this publication meets the minimum requirements of American
National Standard for Information Sciences—Permanence of Paper for Printed Library
Materials, ANSI/NISO Z39.48-1992.

Printed in the United States of America

To all the students I have taught during my
forty-three years at Loyola University Chicago

Contents

Foreword

Sammy Danna has brought us to meet Lydia Pinkham within a rather generous context. We find a good, giving, and spirited woman who has left her kind touch on many lives. Lydia was a resolute woman who sought knowledge and forged lasting relationships. She used both very creatively and with broad impact.

The Vegetable Compound that Lydia formulated appears to assemble ingredients that have some very real medicinal qualities. Or perhaps those ingredients, in their very variety, gave this Vegetable Compound multiple effects that were needed by those using them for a multitude of health concerns. Maybe this was as helpful as medicine could be in the years of its creation and popularity.

Lydia's careful eye and mind were observant of the best knowledge to apply to her fellow women's questions. Her careful heart heard the broader and deeper needs flooding through these women. Some needs were maternal, regarding pregnancy and giving birth; others were concerns of the maturing body. Some women were perplexed over aging or some affliction; others simply desired to be helpful to their sisters, daughters, neighbors, or friends. Each was deserving of her kindness and encouragement.

What a mixture of personalities grew up in the home and under nurture of Lydia and husband Isaac! Each child would be seriously adjusting to accommodate both of their parents. For Dan and Will, their younger sons, life would be short. But through their striving and dreaming, both young men helped make the Vegetable Compound the success it was. By comparison, details of daughter Aroline's personal investment appear less dramatic. But significantly, she brought her husband and family into the Lydia Pinkham Company. However, it fell to son Charles and his wife and children to solidify a long future for the company for which Lydia and the others had laid a broad and deep foundation.

The tradition was handed on and built upon, as the production "family" kept to careful and sanitary ways that ensured an authentic product while actively maintaining correspondence. But for Sammy R. Danna, his interest in the use, effects, and development of advertising communications—indeed of all communicating—there has played out another fascinating and instructive narrative. His gathering of it for the reader will prove a favor.

But no one connected with this narrative is more of a favor than is Lydia herself. She touches everything. She brought fruitfulness through her many interests and loves. She proved to be like the proverbial good wife: knitting together medicinal products and attention to health together with truly human counsel; even her physical attributes and idealized image shone in the homes and families that she called her own. But Lydia is much more than a striking face or a famous portrait. Her product seems to have a certain fountain of youth about it.

Glenn Phillips, OFM, MBA marketing

Acknowledgments

Many individuals and institutions are due my thanks and appreciation for their contributions in creating this book. I will attempt to mention the major acknowledgments but my sincerest apologies to anyone or to any institution I may have forgotten.

To my invaluable graduate assistant, James Andrews, I owe a debt of gratitude beyond mere payment for his consistently faithful services. He has gone beyond the call of duty to weave the many threads of the Lydia Pinkham story. James, I think you are one of a kind. Also, thanks to Brian Donovan, researcher and genealogist, for his extensive research and review on the book; to Michael Limón, nontenure track instructor at Loyola University Chicago's School of Communication, for his excellent work in editing the book; and to Ryan Bedell, Loyola student assistant (now graduated), who was a notable help in research and editing. Thanks also go to Pamela Morris, associate professor at Loyola University Chicago's School of Communication, for her assistance. Also at Loyola, special thanks go to Don Heider, dean of the School of Communication, and Wayne Magdziarz, senior vice president for capital planning and campus management, for their support and encouragement. Thanks also to Olga Corrias Hancock, director of alumni relations, for assisting with Italian translations.

Appreciation also goes to M. Marko, OFS (The Camelot Unit), a longtime Chicago research assistant who analyzed the writing style, and Glenn Phillips, OFM, St. Peter's Church in the Loop, Chicago, who reviewed the book and asked probing questions concerning the Lydia Pinkham story. Thanks go to Virginia Gibbons for proofreading the manuscript.

Thanks to my assistants at Harvard University for their invaluable help in our use of the massive number of Lydia Pinkham Company files at the Radcliff Institute's Schlesinger Library; to John Ulrich, head researcher and senior researcher at Harvard

Student Resources; and his manager, Ali Evans. In addition, thanks also go to Bette Keva, independent researcher, for her work at Harvard. Appreciation is extended for the exceptional research assistance from the Schlesinger librarians, especially to Ellen Shea, Lynda Leahy, Sarah Hutcheon, and Diana Carey. The latter's cooperation, and that of staff assistant Laurie Ellis, was most helpful in accessing Lydia Pinkham's medical notebook.

It is fitting to acknowledge the much-appreciated but completely unsolicited remarks to me from Harvard University's Schlesinger librarians, which occurred after having spent many days of intensive work at the research facility. I was told that the librarians were quite impressed not only with my research but also with how well my assistants worked and responded to my directions.

In addition, thanks go to the Center for the History of Medicine at the Countway Library of Medicine (an alliance of the Boston Medical Library and Harvard University Medical School). Gratitude is expressed to Jack Eckert and Joan Thomas for their online reference work in the summer of 2011 and the fall of 2012, respectively, and to Eckert for assistance in 2014. Also at Countway, Jessica Murphy was especially helpful in a number of ways, specifically providing advice about the controlled use of ether. Harvard's Widener Library provided help as well, as did Columbia University Libraries and the New York Public Library. In Chicago, thanks go to the Loyola University Libraries; Vanessa Crouther, access services supervisor at Lewis Library; and Jennifer Stegen, interlibrary loan librarian at Cudahy Library. Also in Chicago and Evanston, appreciation is extended to the staff at Northwestern University Libraries. In Washington, DC, thanks go to the Library of Congress for special consultations and Paul McCutcheon, senior reference librarian, National Museum of American History at the Smithsonian Institution, for his research and assistance regarding the song "Let Us Sing of Lydia Pinkham." Special thanks go to the staff of *The Dartmouth* student newspaper. At the Dartmouth College Library, thanks go to Rauner special collections librarian Jay Satterfield and to Morgan Swan, PhD, MLIS, special collections education and outreach librarian. Thanks also go to Devin Sanera, reference assistant at Olin and Uris Libraries, Cornell University. Nanci Young, college archivist at Smith College Libraries, deserves thanks for her help regarding Kate Sanborn. At Union College, Schenectady, New York, thanks go to Marlaine DesChamps, archives specialist, for her efforts in tracking down Lydia Pinkham songs.

In Massachusetts, the Lynn Public Library and the Lynn Museum provided rare insights into the life of Lydia Pinkham and the history of her venerable company. At the museum, Steve Babbit, treasurer and trustee, as well as past president of the board, greatly aided my research in 2010 and made available everything of significance that the museum had on Lydia Pinkham. Abby Battis, museum assistant director and curator, read over the manuscript and made suggestions after taking special interest in the project in 2012. I also appreciate her compliment about the thesis being succinct and of the book beging a great read.

In Boston, thanks go to the historic *Boston Herald* Library for its help and consultation on the early Pinkham Company advertisements, which first appeared in the *Herald* in the late 1870s, and to the New England Historic Genealogical Society for aid in determining the Este background of Lydia's family, now known as Estes. Thanks go to Martha Clark, curator at the Massachusetts Archives, for locating William Pinkham's birth registration. Especially useful were the digitized newspaper databases ProQuest, NewsBank, Ancestory.com, FamilySearch, Newspapers.com, Historical Newspapers, Nineteenth Century U.S. Newspapers, JSTOR, and American Historical Periodicals.

These cited works, which are listed in the endnotes, helped make this book possible. For inspiration and insight, I want to acknowledge Sarah Stage's *Female Complaints*, Jean Burton's *Lydia Pinkham Is Her Name*, Robert Collyer Washburn's *Life and Times of Lydia E. Pinkham*, and the dissertation by Elysa Ream Engelman "'The Face That Haunts Me Ever': Consumers, Retailers, Critics, and the Branded Personality of Lydia E. Pinkham." Also important was up-to-date information on Lydia Pinkham herbal remedies provided by Numark Laboratories executives Bob Stites and Moaiz Daya.

Special thank-yous (and love) go to Betty Danna Gilreath and Theresa Danna Coco, who researched Lydia Pinkham illustrations for various portraits and advertisements used in this book.

In addition, I want to recognize Rowman and Littlefield staffers for their help in bringing this work to fruition. Specific acknowledgments go to senior editor Bennett Graff for the cover image and his commitment, concern, and patience; to production editor Andrew Yoder for his fine editing assistance; and to copyeditor Melissa Lind for her numerous suggestions.

One more person who deserves acknowledgment but who did not directly work on the book is Dr. Joseph A. DeVito. His longtime faith in my research and writing efforts has been invaluable. As classmates from the early 1960s at the University of Illinois at Urbana–Champaign, we engaged in doctoral work in rhetoric and public address. Joe, a retired professor from City University of New York, has distinguished himself by publishing many textbooks in the field.

Research on this project began in October 2010 and continued through July 2014. Among the moments I will remember most were when I walked the streets of Lynn and made my way through the factory complex on Western Avenue where Lydia and the rest of the Pinkhams once strode. This affection stayed with me as I visited the family graves in Pine Grove Cemetery, which stand as a testament to lives ventured, with so much lost yet so much gained.

Introduction

Why write on Lydia Pinkham in the first place? She became one of the most remarkable businesswomen of the nineteenth century and a staunch, nonmilitant champion of women's rights and racial equality. Operating in a "man's world," she bucked convention and persuaded thousands of women to believe in and purchase her Vegetable Compound, designed for "female weaknesses" and other more serious illnesses. She evolved into a truly great early woman entrepreneur, perhaps the greatest of her era.

In a period rampant with reckless claims about nonprescription drugs, why did her company's product stand out above the rest and survive to the present day as Lydia Pinkham's Vegetable Compound for Women? It did so through masterful promotion in the time frame of the 1870s to the early 1900s, which emerged as the most prolific and abusive era of patent medicine sales in America. Doctors were expensive and hard to come by for the average family, especially those in sparsely populated areas. As a result, home remedies and patent medicines often were the only alternatives.

The book's theme centers on how Lydia Pinkham, her family, and her associates adeptly used advertising, testimonials, and other related tools to market her compound successfully against long odds, intensive competition, and the fact that in general her product's curative powers were no more than those possessed by the passage of time.

This volume primarily covers the life and times of the Pinkhams, with a focus on Lydia, and to a lesser extent, it brings the reader up to date on the vestiges of Lydia's company. One era is no less important than the other, but in this instance, there is more richness in the past.

1

A Family's Rise in Times of Fortune and Despair

Although Lydia Pinkham may no longer be a household name, and, granted, patent medicines are a concept time has all but forgotten, both live on today, their essence all around. Lydia and her namesake company were pioneers on many levels in the latter half of the 1800s and beyond, from championing issues of social injustice to spearheading advertising breakthroughs and entrepreneurial initiatives. As for patent medicines, they became an industry unto themselves around the time of the Civil War, eventually generating hundreds of millions of dollars in revenue by selling "cure-all" products for a buck a bottle. By the 1860s, potion proprietors were the nation's largest advertisers, and some of their remedies have endured to the twenty-first century under such iconic brands as Vicks VapoRub, Bayer Aspirin, Geritol, Smith Brothers Cough Drops, Carter's Little Liver Pills (now Carter's Laxative), Goody's Powder, and Phillips' Milk of Magnesia.

Less well known today is Lydia's Vegetable Compound, even though a million dollars' worth of the potion is sold every year on the Internet and by word of mouth. But more important than the bottom line is the fact that research has shown the compound may have been one hundred years ahead of its time when it hit the market in 1875, promising relief from menstrual ailments. That the often-mocked remedy actually had a hint of therapeutic power wouldn't be a surprise to anyone who knew Lydia, given her knack for pushing boundaries and her family's history of confronting one intense challenge after another.

Lydia Estes Pinkham was born on February 9, 1819, in Lynn, Massachusetts, the tenth of a dozen children in the Billy Estes family. Lydia's children later managed to trace their ancestry to the thirteenth-century Italian House of Este.[1] Because of political differences, the ancestors were forced into exile in England and remained there for four centuries.

The Estes history was rich on both sides of the Atlantic, on the one hand touching the halls of power and on other treading through the struggles of the common man. Through an imperial lineage dating from 500 B.C. to latter-day links with royalty and statesmen, the Estes arch spanned eras and historic episodes. In Europe, the ties may have stretched to everyone from Byzantine emperors to Christopher Columbus, who shared a lineage to the House of Paleologus and therefore claimed, "I am a Byzantine prince." Once in America, the ties continued to notable pioneer families, their branches spreading to many states. They played a part in many historical events, including the American Revolution and the Civil War, which found members fighting on both sides. A few even gained political prominence, including U.S. Senator Estes Kefauver (1903–1963), a candidate for vice president (1956).

Going back hundreds of years, the Estes thread reached to Manuel II, the last emperor of Constantinople, whose Paleologus family ruled from 1282 A.D. to 1453 A.D. The House of Paleologus also could claim to be heirs of the Kingdom of Cypress and Jerusalem, but with the fall of Constantinople in 1453, the various branches of the royal family fled and took refuge in nations throughout Europe. One branch landed in Italy, where it found its way to Tivoli, almost twenty miles northeast of Rome, and built Villa d'Este, which today is a tourist and showplace destination. The family joined the Catholic Church to avoid persecution, and later two family members became cardinals. But it could not avoid the political infighting sweeping the country and eventually was exiled.[2]

Nicholas Estes was among the first recorded generation of Estes in England, born in 1495 in Deal, Kent. He married in 1520, and the lineage descends from him.[3] In 1676, Matthew Estes migrated to America, which produced an eminent family line that included Lydia Pinkham.[4]

In the late eighteenth century, Lydia's father, Billy Estes, began his career as a shoemaker, commonly known in his day as a cordwainer. Lynn was earning the name the "city of shoes," but when the War of 1812 erupted, Billy created a saltworks on the flatlands near his home, an investment that paid off well for the Estes family. No longer a cordwainer when business recessions created difficulties for the trades, Billy owned a large farm in the path of the city's development when Lydia was born. Dealing in real estate, Billy amassed a small fortune.[5]

Their times of plenty, however, were not always times of tranquility. Controversy often was a companion because of the people and causes with which they associated. In 1842, Lydia's older sister, Gulielma Maria, came under fire from the Methodist Church because of her friendship with Frederick Douglass (1818–1895), a renowned black abolitionist leader.

From an early age, Lydia believed in reform, such as abolishing slavery, and at sixteen became a charter member of the Lynn Female Anti-Slavery Society, along with her mother and older sister. The group also was heavily invested in a women's rights crusade.[6]

On the surface, the Estes family and Douglass might have seemed unlikely allies. He was born a slave in ca. 1818 who barely knew his mother because they lived on separate plantations until her death when he was only seven. But through several twists of fate, by the time Douglass reached his early twenties, he and Lydia's family lived in the same Lynn neighborhood and shared a passion for opposing almost any type of discrimination.

Douglass's lifelong battles and his eloquent but determined way of fighting back hardened the resolve of those who came into his sphere of influence. His experiences became a source of well-told talking points that served as inspiration to reformers and a counterpoint to those who said blacks lacked intellectual capacity. On the plantation, he experienced slavery's brutality, but in 1825, he was sent to live with relatives of his master's wife in Baltimore.[7] Life initially was better, but Douglass vowed he would one day be free. At an early age, he had absorbed a great deal of knowledge, and by twelve, he had taught himself to read.[8] Douglass said, "If a slave has a bad master, his ambition is to get a better [master]. When he gets a better [master], he aspires to have the best [master]. And when he gets the best, he aspires to be his own master."[9]

Douglass attempted to escape in 1836 but failed.[10] While focusing on his education and the pursuit of knowledge, he joined the East Baltimore Mental Improvement Society, where he met his future wife, Anna Murray.[11] Within two years, Douglass escaped slavery and continued to educate himself while on the path to becoming a leader in the antislavery movement.[12] He also married, and the couple moved to Lynn in 1841, setting up their friendship with the Estes and Pinkham families.

Trouble came in 1845, when Douglass's former owner set out to enslave him again. Douglass went on the run, and in a letter published in the *Boston Daily Advertiser*, he made no apologies to the authorities seeking his capture.[13] To combat the situation, he fled to England, where friends purchased his freedom for $150.[14] While abroad, he found much less prejudice in Europe and wrote about his experiences, which found their way into American newspapers.[15] In England, people recognized Douglass as a man and never a slave.[16] When he returned to America, he settled in Rochester, New York, and started publishing the *North Star*, an antislavery newspaper.[17] Although Douglass often spoke critically of his former master, the two reconciled after he learned the master had abolished slavery on his plantation.[18]

During his life, Douglass became a well-known speaker, writer, and advocate for the abolishment of slavery, as well as a women's suffrage supporter.[19] He argued that women should have the right to own and sell property, the right to work for equal wages, and the right to vote.[20] Although his allegiances to both causes led to conflicts with female suffragists, he will be remembered as a prominent supporter of women's rights.[21]

A less-well-known fact about Douglass was that he, like Lydia and her family, was a strong temperance movement supporter throughout his life.[22] In a speech, Douglass asserted, "I am here to say, that all drunkenness is traceable to the drinking system of society."[23] But it was his push for racial equality that dominated his activism. Even after slavery was abolished, Douglass said, "My mission for the present is to ask equal citizenship in the state and equal fellowship for the Negro in the church. Equal rights in the street cars and equal admission in the state schools."[24] According to an article in the *Liberator* newspaper in June 1844, Douglass even denounced organized religion for its racial prejudice.[25]

From the beginning of the Civil War, Douglass, in his speeches and writings, urged President Lincoln to pass an emancipation proclamation, his reasoning being that thousands of willing black men would fight for the Union army.[26] After Lincoln issued the executive order, Douglass focused on recruiting black soldiers and championing their rights.[27]

Because Gulielma Estes often associated with Douglass after his move to Lynn, her church congregation asked her to leave. The Rev. Jacob Sanborn declared her actions scandalous after the abolitionist *Liberator* and *Herald of Freedom* newspapers reported that she was walking with Douglass and taking his arm. The reverend asked Gulielma if she was "much acquainted with 'colored people.'" She responded, "Not as much as I hope to be." Later, he asked her to stand before the congregation and "confess that she had been imprudent in being in the company of colored men in the 'manner' which she acknowledges, and promise that she will do so no more . . . or her connection with the Church must be dissolved." Gulielma did not accept the invitation.[28]

As those events were unfolding, Lydia was following similar paths while charting new ones of her own. She absorbed abolitionist ideas and learned about progressive teaching methods from her grammar school instructor, Alonzo Lewis (1794–1861), one of Lynn's leading intellectuals. In addition to later teaching at Lynn Academy secondary school and becoming its principal, Lewis edited a Lynn-based antislavery newspaper.[29]

Lydia took Lewis's concepts into her repertoire while chasing a longtime dream of becoming a teacher.[30] After grammar school, she graduated from Lynn Academy with honors, a rarity for most other women of the time.[31] Throughout, Lydia also was gathering information about remedies for medical ailments, an ongoing pursuit that would one day be the foundation of the Pinkham family's patent medicine empire.

With her abolitionist ideas in place, Lydia and the Estes family always welcomed Douglass into their home. Lydia also taught Douglass's wife, Anna Murray, reading skills.[32]

As a black American, Douglass was forced into the segregated Jim Crow car whenever he rode the train. On September 28, 1841, Douglass decided to pay for a first-class ticket and board the "white car." The conductor, along with other individuals, instructed him to move. Because he viewed the Jim Crow car as part of slaveholding prejudice, he stood his ground before being removed by force.[33] Another time, Lydia reportedly accompanied him in the "white car," and once again Douglass was removed but not before Lydia stood in the conductor's way.[34] Douglass's efforts could be seen to have presaged those of Rosa Parks and her refusal to give up her seat on a bus in the 1950s.[35]

Douglass was not the only notable figure who lived in Lydia's neighborhood at the time. Others include suffragette Susan B. Anthony (1820–1906) and Mary Baker

Eddy (1821–1910), best known for founding Christian Science and launching *The Christian Science Monitor.*[36] Eddy, who was linked to the Estes family through a land transaction, shared Lydia's penchant for investigating health matters and avoiding medical treatments of the day. Eddy experimented with placebos and found that a patient's beliefs played a big role in the healing process. Even with her extensive scientific research, Eddy always held the Bible in high regard. In 1866, she fell on an icy sidewalk, winding up in the hospital in critical condition. She did little but study the Bible as she lay in bed, and while reading a passage on Jesus's healing, she said she instantly felt well. This solidified her faith in Christian Science, or the belief of divine healing.[37]

For Lydia's part, even as she toiled away as a schoolteacher while living at home, the future entrepreneur also managed to be very social, attending many public events. One group she could not avail herself of was the Lynn debating society, which didn't allow women members, so Lydia helped create the rival Freeman's Institute. She described its beginning: "On the evening of January 19, 1843, . . . an assembly of persons, male and female, met at Richards Hall to consider the fitness of uniting in an association for the free discussion of such subjects as might be deemed worthy of remark, untrammeled by the usual rules and forms of debating societies." On the following day, Lydia Estes was nominated and chosen as secretary.[38]

The Freeman's Institute not only advocated abolitionist viewpoints but pressed for gender equality. Douglass was elected president, and Lydia transcribed the constitution, which stated, "No person shall be excluded from full participation in any of the operations of this society on account of sex, complexion, or religious or political opinions." The group had ninety members, including twenty-seven women.[39]

Through the organization, Lydia met Isaac Pinkham, with whom she shared a great many interests. Pinkham's background was similar and his lineage notable. Ancestor Richard Pinkham, or Pinkhame, was a signatory to the first formal government at Dover Point, New Hampshire, in 1640.[40]

Isaac was born on Christmas Day in 1815 in Portsmouth, New Hampshire.[41] Before meeting Lydia, he dabbled in short careers as a kerosene manufacturer, trader, farmer, produce dealer, real estate operator, and perhaps even tried the whale oil business.[42] When Lydia and Isaac met, he worked as a shoe manufacturer, and he also was a widower. His first wife, Mary Shaw of Lynn, had died a year earlier, survived by two daughters, one of whom died shortly thereafter.[43]

When Lydia and Isaac met, she was twenty-four, and he was twenty-seven.[44] Lydia was five foot, ten inches, with red hair and strong, dark eyes. Isaac was short, mild mannered, and very polite. He seemed most interested in making lots of money, with business always on his mind.[45] They married September 8, 1843, but even after their union, the pair did not settle down.[46] Instead, they both continued their work and acquired new responsibilities, although finances apparently were an issue. Lydia's father lent the couple money so they could buy their first home, and when he died in 1848, Isaac began selling off their land inheritance in lots. This seemed to be a promising venture because the railroads operated tracks through their property. Isaac was convinced that the area would eventually become Lynn's business district. His prediction was right, but his timing was poor. The couple lacked available cash and could no longer afford to live in their own house, so they were forced to move into a two-family residence in Wyoma Village on the outskirts of Lynn.[47]

In 1844, the couple welcomed their first son, Charles Hacker.[48] Lydia gave birth to another child, Daniel Rogers, in 1846, but he lived only about a year.[49] They gave the same name to their next child, born in 1848.[50] William Henry, born in 1852, was the youngest male Pinkham.[51] The family's financial troubles persisted, prompting a move to nearby Bedford, Massachusetts, which was deemed more affordable. Their only daughter, Aroline Chase, was born there in 1857.[52]

To help with finances, Charles years later would drop out of school. But thanks to a few wise investments by Isaac, the family's fortunes eventually took a positive swing, allowing the Pinkhams to return to Lynn before the Civil War. All the while, Lydia encouraged her children to work hard in school and apply their brains. Thanks to her tutoring, the remaining brood had very successful high school careers.[53]

Besides conducting her motherly duties, Lydia was known as a very good neighbor. Because of her high level of education, she often was thrust into the role of nurse, her opinion valued when it came to health matters. For years, through her studies and by way of the Estes family, she had collected a number of remedies to combat sickness.[54]

"Medical Directions for Ailments," a notebook written in her own hand, contained numerous folk remedies. Some were common in the day, while others would seem far from normal at any time: "A hog's milt procured fresh from the slaughter house split in halves, one half to be bound on the sole of each foot and allowed to remain there until perfectly dry, will produce relief and in many cases effect a cure of the complaint called asthma."[55]

Lydia transcribed descriptions of the troubles affecting not only women she knew but those who wrote to her as the popularity of her treatments grew by word of mouth. She then recorded her recommendations, such as one to Mary Popple Eagleville, who had trouble with her kidneys. Lydia had prescribed a vegetable concoction and two medicinal herbs—Jacob's ladder and heartsease—a potion that of course later would figure prominently in the Pinkham family's lives.[56]

Lynn during this time had become a bustling community,[57] whose fortunes were partly built on the sales of rum.[58] In a town rife with alcohol, the Pinkhams ostensibly fell on the side of temperance movements, most of which demonized consumption. But when it came to health matters, the family would later join others outside the movements who saw value in liquor for "medicinal purposes."[59] In fact, the Vegetable Compound would feature an alcohol content of 18 percent. Although booze would become a crucial commodity for the Pinkhams down the road in the years after the Civil War, their fortunes were again tied to real estate, as land values in Lynn soared.

Seeking to take advantage of the optimism, by 1872, Isaac in essence had become a land speculator, constantly borrowing against sizable holdings. Next, he was a building contractor, constructing rows of houses that sold very quickly. He even developed Pinkham Hall, a business block complete with an auditorium on the second floor. Also, by cashing in some of his profits, he was able to move the family into one of the best homes in one of Lynn's finest neighborhoods. The trouble was, because inflation had made loans ridiculously easy to obtain, Isaac was operating only on credit and always had to borrow money at high interest rates.[60]

Through his ups and downs of investing in combustible enterprises, Isaac created a list of principles, "To Secure Success in Business," which he passed on to his sons:

1. Make all your purchases, as far as possible, [from] those who stand the highest in uprightness and integrity. Men of character.
2. Enter into no business arrangements with anyone unless you are well satisfied that such person is governed by a strict sense of honor and justice.
3. Engage in nothing of business at arms' length, and be sure you are well acquainted with whatever business you may engage in.
4. Be satisfied with doing well and continue well doing. A sure sixpence is better than a doubtful shilling, which motto, be governed by.[61]

Considering his track record, it is debatable how well Isaac followed his own rules. Later, when it came to building the Pinkham family business, Lydia's sons deviated a great deal from the principles, instead following their own beliefs.

In their youth, the Pinkham boys faced and generally overcame a series of hardships that not only helped shape them but prepared them to deal with family misfortunes. Little is known about Charles, the eldest, before 1882. At age seventeen, he enlisted in the Union Army and was assigned to Fortress Monroe for guard duty. He reenlisted and saw fighting on a grand scale after General Robert E. Lee's retreat at the Battle of Gettysburg. Charles returned to Lynn after his honorable discharge and became one of the first conductors on the new Lynn and Boston Railroad. He was ambitious, but his family's financial situation held those aspirations in check until later in his life.[62]

Although the Pinkhams' second child died in infancy, his name lived on through their third child, Daniel Rogers, after Lydia's longtime friend, Nathaniel Rogers (1794–1846).[63] This son was often called the "brilliant" member of the family after graduating at the top of his class at Lynn High School in 1866.[64] Dan performed well in school, was generally successful in business and politics, and was central to the family's triumphs in later years. But at nearly every stop along the way, either the Pinkhams' missteps or their tightly held convictions seemed to derail him. The family's chronic lack of cash forced him to borrow textbooks from fellow students, yet he was chosen to deliver the valedictory address on the topic "The Right of Suffrage."[65]

Always resourceful, he scraped together enough money to travel to the "Wild West," getting work in Missouri and Kansas before joining an expedition through the Indian Territory (Oklahoma) to Texas. While on the road, he contracted a serious illness but managed to recover then supported himself for a time by teaching at a Texas school.[66]

By 1871, Dan had returned to Lynn and worked odd jobs to help the family. At only twenty-two, he conducted himself in a very mature manner, and although he had political aspirations, financial pressures put them on hold. Dan operated a neighborhood grocery store with only moderate success before it eventually failed, partly because he refused to stock liquor.[67] Jobs as a letter carrier and postal clerk connected him with the public, aiding his eventual entry into politics and his later efforts to promote the family's business.[68] In 1876, Dan ran for office and was elected, representing Ward 1 in the common council. Three years later, he was elected to the Massachusetts Legislature and became a leader in the Greenback and Labor movements. The Greenback Party was a political organization founded in 1874 whose chief concern was opposing the reduction of paper money.[69] As a politician, Dan worked hard and gave speeches representing his beliefs and those of the Greenbacks.[70]

Dan soon became known as the Legislature's "fish-ball" because he advocated that members' salaries be cut to $350 from $650. In a speech, he said his colleagues should come down to a "fish-ball diet." Running for a second term, he was defeated by a newcomer in politics, Henry Cabot Lodge (1850–1924), who had the backing of liquor interests.[71]

The Pinkhams' youngest son, Will, like Dan, was a good student, becoming the high school class valedictorian in 1870. Will apparently was the most outgoing brother and everyone's favorite. His sense of optimism matched Lydia's and was conveyed in his valedictorian speech:

> As education is being promoted so that everything in the universe became useful to mankind is progressing. . . . The improvement in traveling is not the least of the miracles which steam has wrought. By its potent agency one rushes from Boston to San Francisco almost with the speed of the wind. What remains to be accomplished by the power of electricity, an agency not yet understood, time only will determine.[72]

Will's goal to enter Harvard fell victim to Isaac's wild ambitions. Instead, Will taught at a Quaker academy in Weare, New Hampshire, and in the late 1870s became a grammar school principal in Bedford. He later made invaluable contributions to the family business.[73]

For a time, Isaac and others in the business world rode the real estate boom of the early 1870s. Believing that land prices had not peaked, he chose not to cash in and hoped to double his income. Instead, he was betrayed by his overconfidence and trusting nature. When he obliged others by endorsing their promissory notes, he was left without funds to cover his debts when they came due.[74]

The beginning of the end for many investors was the Panic of 1873. Isaac lost almost everything when it struck. Overnight, just one week after Lydia and Isaac celebrated their thirtieth wedding anniversary, land values dropped dramatically, banks closed, and most people became too cautious to buy or build.[75] Thousands in Lynn and hundreds of thousands elsewhere lost their jobs. In New York, the stock exchange closed for ten days.[76]

Within a week, a bank officer came to arrest Isaac, only to find him sick in bed. The attorney pressing charges turned out to be a distant relative and dropped the suit. Although spared embarrassment, Isaac was never the same, his enthusiasm and vitality spent. Arthur Pinkham, recalling this time with his grandfather, related, "He was a feeble old man, rocking in a chair by the fire."[77] Author Earle Stern, who engaged in an extensive study of the Pinkham family, described Isaac as someone "who became both insolvent and a semi-invalid" after the 1873 crash.[78]

It would be up to the other Pinkhams to find salvation, and it would be up to Lydia to assume the role of heroine.

NOTES

1. Lydia Estes, birth (February 9, 1819), Vital Records of Lynn Massachusetts to the End of the Year 1849, vol. 1, Births (Salem, MA: Essex Institute, 1905), 140, Ancestry.com, Massachusetts, Town and Vital Records, 1620–1988 [online database] (Provo, UT: Ancestry.com Operations, 2011). Original data: Town and City Clerks of Massachusetts, Massachusetts Vital and Town Records (Provo, UT: Holbrook Research Institute, Jay and Delene Holbrook), http://search.ancestry.com/search/db.aspx?dbid=2495.

2. "Estes," Ancestry.com, http://freepages.genealogy.rootsweb.ancestry.com/~fdmoore/estes.htm; and "Was Columbus Greek," Greece Travel.com, http://www.greecetravel.com/history/columbus/.

3. Ibid.

4. Charles Estes, Estes Genealogies 1097–1893 (Salem, MA: Eben Putnam, 1894), 1–28.

5. Paul Gustaf Faler, "Workingmen, Mechanics and Social Change: Lynn, Massachusetts 1800–1860" (Ph.D. diss., University of Wisconsin, 1971), 51; Alan Dawley, *Class and Community: The Industrial Revolution in Lynn* (Cambridge, MA: Harvard University Press, 1976), 51–56; and Sarah Stage, *Female Complaints: Lydia Pinkham and the Business of Women's Medicine* (New York: Norton, 1979), 18.

6. "Clerical Impudence—The Climax," from the *Liberator*, quoted in the *Herald of Freedom*, September 2, 1842, n.p.; and Stage, *Female Complaints*, 21.

7. William B. Rogers, *We Are All Together Now* (New York: Garland, 1995), 87–88.

8. Barbara Bennett Woodhouse, *Hidden in Plain Sight* (Princeton, NJ: Princeton University Press, 2008), 56–57; and Wilson Jeremiah Moses, *Creative Conflict in African American Thought* (New York: Cambridge University Press, 2004), 37.

9. Rogers, *We Are All Together*, 89.

10. Ibid.

11. Ibid.

12. Ibid., 90.

13. Frederick Douglass, "Letter from Frederick Douglass," *Boston Daily Advertiser*, no. 108, November 4, 1859; Douglass, *Narrative*, 146; and Peter Burchard, *Frederick Douglass for the Great Family of Man* (New York: Atheneum Books for Young Readers, 2003), 79.

14. Wade Hudson, *Powerful Words* (New York: Scholastic, 2004), 29.

15. "Miscellany: Letter from Frederick Douglass," *Barre Patriot* (Barre, MA), vol. 2, no. 33, March 3, 1846, 1.

16. [No Title], *Berkshire County Whig* (Pittsfield, MA), vol. 6, no. 265, April 4, 1846, 2.

17. Hudson, *Powerful Words*, 29.

18. "To Capt. Thomas Alud, Formerly My Master," *Liberator* (Boston), no. 37, September 14, 1849, 146, col. B.

19. Frederick Douglass, *Woman's Journal* (April 14, 1888), available online at "(1888) Frederick Douglass on Woman Suffrage," BlackPast.org, http://www.blackpast.org/1888-frederick-douglass-woman-suffrage.

20. Burchard, *Frederick Douglass*, 118.

21. C. C. O'Brien, "'The White Women All Go for Sex': Frances Harper on Suffrage, Citizenship, and the Reconstruction South," *African American Review* 43, no. 4 (Winter 2009): 605–8.

22. Rogers, *We Are All Together*, 96.

23. "Speech of Frederick Douglass, Recently Delivered at a Large Temperance Meeting in London," *Journal of the American Temperance Union* 9, no. 1 (January 1845): 140, col. 3.

24. Carol Faulkner, *Women's Radical Reconstruction: The Freedmen's Aid Movement* (Philadelphia: University of Pennsylvania Press, 2004), 69; and William S. McFeely, *Frederick Douglass* (New York: W. W. Norton, 1991), 242.

25. [No Title], *Liberator* (Boston), no. 24, June 14, 1844, col. F, 19th Century U.S. Newspapers.

26. Burchard, *Frederick Douglass*, 148.

27. Ibid., 153.

28. "Clerical Impudence—The Climax," from the *Liberator*, quoted in the *Herald of Freedom*, September 2, 1842, n.p.

29. "Literature Trail: Alonzo Lewis and Lynn Writers," *Escapes North*, http://www.escapes-north.com/trail_lit/trail.php?sec=&trail=23; and Jean Burton, *Lydia Pinkham Is Her Name* (New York: Little and Ives, 1949), 13.

30. Burton, *Lydia Pinkham*, 13; Stage, *Female Complaints*, 24; and Elbert Hubbard, *Lydia E. Pinkham: Being a Sketch of Her Life and Times* (East Aurora, NY: Roycrofters, 1915), 18.

31. Nancy M. Theriot, *Mothers and Daughters in Nineteenth-Century America* (Lexington, KY: The University Press of Kentucky, 1996), 79–80; and Burton, *Lydia Pinkham*, 14.

32. Burton, *Lydia Pinkham*, 21; and Stage, *Female Complaints*, 22.

33. Frederick Douglass, *Life and Times of Frederick Douglass* (Boston: De Wolfe, Fiske, 1893), 277.

34. Ibid.; Burton, *Lydia Pinkham*, 20–22; and Robert Collyer Washburn, *The Life and Times of Lydia Pinkham* (New York: G. P. Putnam's Sons, 1931), 31.

35. "Rosa Parks Biography," *Academy of Achievement*, http://www.achievement.org/autodoc/page/par0bio-1.

36. Ann Anderson, *Snake Oil, Hustlers, and Hambones: The American Medicine Show* (Jefferson, NC: McFarland, 2000), 36.

37. "Mary Baker Eddy," *Mary Baker Eddy Library*, http://www.marybakereddylibrary.org/mary-baker-eddy/life.

38. Minutes of the Freemans Institute from January 19, 1843, recorded by Lydia Pinkham, secretary, "Notebook of Lydia E. Pinkham, Including Minutes of Freemans Institute, 1848–1865," folder 3365, frame 14 of seventy-seven scans in the author's possession, The Lydia E. Pinkham Medicine Company Records, Schlesinger Library, Radcliffe Institute, Harvard University; and Burton, Lydia Pinkham, 22.

39. Minutes of the Freemans Institute from January 19, 1843; and   Burton, Lydia Pinkham, 23.

40. Burton, *Lydia Pinkham*, 25.

41. Isaac Pinkham (1815–1889), detail photograph of Pinkham memorial by Alex (no. 47424643), Find A Grave Memorial, no. 67034744 for Isaac Pinkham, http://www.findagrave.com/cgi-bin/fg.cgi?page=gr&GRid=67034744, accessed September 8, 2014; and "Massachusetts, Births and Christenings, 1639–1915," index, FamilySearch (https://familysearch.org/pal:/MM9.1.1/VQXG-2Q5), Daniel Rogers Pinkham, (November 19, 1848); citing LYNN, ESSEX, MASSACHUSETTS, FHL microfilm 0397791 V. 1; and Daniel Rogers Pinkham, birth (November 19, 1848), Vital Records of Lynn Massachusetts to the End of the Year 1849, vol. 1, Births (Salem, MA: Essex Institute, 1905), 326, Ancestry.com, Massachusetts, Town and Vital Records 1620–1988 [online database] (Provo, UT: Ancestry.com Operations, 2011). Original data: Town and City Clerks of Massachusetts, Massachusetts Vital and Town Records (Provo, UT: Holbrook Research Institute, Jay and Delene Holbrook), http://search.ancestry.com/search/db.aspx?dbid=2495.

42. Bob Trieger, "Lydia Pinkham Sold an Image," *The Daily Item* (Lynn, MA), April 6, 1999, 6.

43. "Massachusetts, Deaths, 1841–1915," index and images, FamilySearch (https://familysearch.org/pal:/MM9.1.1/N7JR-F2P), Mary Pinkham (August 30, 1842); citing Lynn, Massachusetts, 160, State Archives, Boston; FHL microfilm 1420527; "Massachusetts, Deaths, 1841-1915," index and images, FamilySearch (https://familysearch.org/pal:/MM9.1.1/N7JR-FP2), Mary Adaline Pinkham, (September 24, 1842); citing Lynn, Massachusetts, 160, State Archives, Boston; FHL microfilm 1420527; and Mary [Shaw] and Mary Adaline Pinkham, deaths (August 30, 1842, and September 24, 1842, respectively), Vital Records of Lynn Massachusetts to the End of the Year 1849, vol. 2, Marriages and Deaths (Salem, MA: Essex Institute, 1906), 564, Ancestry.com, Massachusetts, Town and Vital Records, 1620–1988 [online database] (Provo, UT: Ancestry.com Operations, 2011). Original data: Town and City Clerks of Massachusetts, Massachusetts Vital and Town Records (Provo, UT: Holbrook Research Institute, Jay and Delene Holbrook), http://search.ancestry.com/search/db.aspx?dbid=2495.

44. Based on the year the Freeman's Institute was founded and when Mary Pinkham died were utilized to calculate the most likely ages of Lydia and Isaac when they met.

45. Ibid., 22, 28; and Washburn, *Life and Times*, 54.

46. "Vermont, Vital Records, 1760–1954," index and images, FamilySearch (https://familysearch.org/pal:/MM9.1.1/XFJL-M68), Isaac Pinkham and Lydia Estes (September 8, 1843), Marriage; State Capitol Building, Montpelier; FHL microfilm 27542; "Vermont, Vital Records, 1760–1954," index and images, FamilySearch (https://familysearch.org/pal:/MM9.1.1/V8ML-SHD), Isaac Pinkham and Lydia Estes, (September 8, 1843), Marriage; State Capitol Building, Montpelier; FHL microfilm 27657; and Isaac Pinkham and Lydia Estes, marriage card index, Rockingham County, Vermont (September 8, 1841), Ancestry.com, Vermont, Vital Records, 1720–1908 [online database] (Provo, UT: Ancestry.com Operations, 2013). Original data: State of Vermont, Vermont Vital Records through 1870 (Boston: New England Historic Genealogical Society); and State of Vermont, Vermont Vital Records, 1871–1908 (Boston: New England Historic Genealogical Society), http://search.ancestry.com/search/db.aspx?dbid=4661.

47. Burton, *Lydia Pinkham*, 29–30; "Massachusetts, Deaths and Burials, 1795–1910," index, FamilySearch (https://familysearch.org/pal:/MM9.1.1/FH6L-F31), William Estes, (March 3, 1848); citing reference item 4 p 137; FHL microfilm 1927788; William Estes, death (March 3, 1848), Vital Records of Lynn Massachusetts to the End of the Year 1849, vol. 2, Marriages and Deaths (Salem, MA: Essex Institute, 1906), 564, Ancestry.com; Massa-

chusetts, Death Records, 1841–1915 [online database] (Provo, UT: Ancestry.com Operations, 2013. Original data: Massachusetts Vital Records, 1840–1911 (Boston: New England Historic Genealogical Society); and Massachusetts Vital Records, 1911–1915 (Boston: New England Historic Genealogical Society), http://search.ancestry.com/search/db.aspx?dbid=2495.

48. "Massachusetts, Births and Christenings, 1639-1915," index, FamilySearch (https://familysearch.org/pal:/MM9.1.1/VQXG-BFC), Charles H. Pinkham (December 23, 1844); citing LYNN,ESSEX,MASSACHUSETTS; FHL microfilm 0397791 V. 1; and Charles H. Pinkham, birth (December 23, 1844), Vital Records of Lynn Massachusetts to the End of the Year 1849, vol. 1, Births (Salem, MA: Essex Institute, 1905), 326, Ancestry.com, Massachusetts, Town and Vital Records, 1620–1988 [online database] (Provo, UT: Ancestry.com Operations, 2011). Original data: Town and City Clerks of Massachusetts, Massachusetts Vital and Town Records (Provo, UT: Holbrook Research Institute, Jay and Delene Holbrook), http://search.ancestry.com/search/db.aspx?dbid=2495.

49. "Massachusetts, Births and Christenings, 1639–1915," index, FamilySearch (https://familysearch.org/pal:/MM9.1.1/VQXG-2QL), Daniel R. Pinkham, (July 7, 1846); citing LYNN,ESSEX,MASSACHUSETTS; FHL microfilm 0397791 V. 1; Daniel R. Pinkham, birth (July 7, 1846), Vital Records of Lynn Massachusetts to the End of the Year 1849, vol. 1, Births (Salem, MA: Essex Institute, 1905), 326, Ancestry.com, Massachusetts, Town and Vital Records, 1620–1988 [online database] (Provo, UT: Ancestry.com Operations, 2011). Original data: Town and City Clerks of Massachusetts, Massachusetts Vital and Town Records (Provo, UT: Holbrook Research Institute, Jay and Delene Holbrook). Source information:. Massachusetts, http://search.ancestry.com/search/db.aspx?dbid=2495; and "Massachusetts, Deaths, 1841–1915," index and images, FamilySearch (https://familysearch.org/pal:/MM9.1.1/NWCL-336), Daniel R. Pinkham, (August 27, 1847); citing Lynn, Essex, Massachusetts, v 32 p 99, State Archives, Boston; FHL microfilm 959810; and Daniel Rogers Pinkham, death (August 27, 1847), Vital Records of Lynn Massachusetts to the End of the Year 1849, vol. 2, Marriages and Deaths (Salem, MA: Essex Institute, 1906), 564, Ancestry.com, Massachusetts, Death Records, 1841–1915 [online database] (Provo, UT: Ancestry.com Operations, 2013). Original data: Massachusetts Vital Records, 1840–1911 (Boston: New England Historic Genealogical Society); and Massachusetts Vital Records, 1911–1915 (Boston: New England Historic Genealogical Society), http://search.ancestry.com/search/db.aspx?dbid=2101.

50. "Massachusetts, Births and Christenings, 1639–1915," index, FamilySearch (https://familysearch.org/pal:/MM9.1.1/VQXG-2Q5), Daniel Rogers Pinkham, (November 19 1848); citing LYNN,ESSEX,MASSACHUSETTS; FHL microfilm 0397791 V. 1; and Daniel Rogers Pinkham, birth (November 19, 1848), Vital Records of Lynn Massachusetts to the End of the Year 1849, vol. 1, Births (Salem, MA: Essex Institute, 1905), 326, Ancestry.com, Massachusetts, Town and Vital Records, 1620–1988 [online database] (Provo, UT: Ancestry.com Operations, 2011). Original data: Town and City Clerks of Massachusetts, Massachusetts Vital and Town Records (Provo, UT: Holbrook Research Institute, Jay and Delene Holbrook), http://search.ancestry.com/search/db.aspx?dbid=2495.

51. "Massachusetts, Births, 1841–1915," index and images, FamilySearch (https://familysearch.org/pal:/MM9.1.1/FXCW-G86), Pinkham, (December 30, 1852); citing Lynn, Essex, Massachusetts, 203, Massachusetts Archives, Boston; FHL microfilm 1420835; Male [William Henry] Pinkham, birth registration no. 442 (December 30), "Births Registered in the City of Lynn, for the Year 1852," Massachusetts Vital Records, 1841–1940, vol. 63, Births 1852, 203, microfilm no. 1,420,835, frame 207, Family History Library, Salt Lake City, UT. Source Information: Ancestry.com. Massachusetts, Death Records, 1841–1915 [online

database] (Provo, UT: Ancestry.com Operations, 2013). Original data: Massachusetts Vital Records, 1840–1911 (Boston: New England Historic Genealogical Society); and Massachusetts Vital Records, 1911–1915 (Boston: New England Historic Genealogical Society), http://search.ancestry.com/search/db.aspx?dbid=2101.

52. Aroline Pinkham, birth (June 7, 1857), Bedford, Middlesex County, Massachusetts, Index to Births in Massachusetts 1856–1860, unpaginated, vol. 106, 60, Ancestry.com, Massachusetts, Town and Vital Records, 1620–1988 [online database] (Provo, UT: Ancestry.com Operations, 2011). Original data: Town and City Clerks of Massachusetts, Massachusetts Vital and Town Records (Provo, UT: Holbrook Research Institute, Jay and Delene Holbrook), http://search.ancestry.com/search/db.aspx?dbid=2495.

53. Burton, *Lydia Pinkham*, 33–34; and Stage, *Female Complaints*, 28.

54. Burton, *Lydia Pinkham*, 36–37. Lydia Pinkham, "Medical Directions for Ailments," ca. 1878, vol. 537, The Lydia E. Pinkham Medicine Company Records, Schlesinger Library, Radcliffe Institute, Harvard University.

55. Lydia Pinkham, "Medical Directions for Ailments," ca. 1878, vol. 537, 72–73. The Lydia E. Pinkham Medicine Company Records, Schlesinger Library, Radcliffe Institute, Harvard University.

56. Ibid., 3.

57. Alonzo Lewis and James R. Newhall, *History of Lynn, Essex County Massachusetts, Including Lynnfield, Saugus, Swampscot, and Nahant* (Boston: John L. Shorey, 1865), 590–592.

58. Washburn, *Life and Times*, 23–24; and "The Coming of Drink to New England (1620–1820)," Maine Historical Society, http://www.mainehistory.org/rum-riot-reform/1620-1820/index.html.

59. Burton, *Lydia Pinkham*, 63–65; and Stage, *Female Complaints*, 32.

60. Ibid., 58–59, 65–66; and *The Lynn Directory 1871*, Boston: Sampson, Davenport, 1871, 216.

61. Lydia E. Pinkham, "Journal of Lydia E. Pinkham," box 180, folder 3365, The Lydia E. Pinkham Medicine Company Records, Schlesinger Library, Radcliffe Institute, Harvard University; and Stage, Female Complaints, 26–27.

62. Charles H. Pinkham, "Advertising 1875–1953," 1953, 6, The Lydia E. Pinkham Medicine Company Records, Schlesinger Library, Radcliffe Institute, Harvard University.

63. Stage, *Female Complaints*, 25.

64. C. H. Pinkham, "Advertising 1875–1953," 6.

65. Burton, *Lydia Pinkham*, 59–60; and Daniel Rogers Pinkham, valedictorian speech, "Right of Suffrage," in Lydia E. Pinkham, "Notebook of Lydia E. Pinkham, Including Minutes of Freemans Institute, 1848–1865," folder 3365, frame 75 of seventy-seven scans in the author's possession.

66. C. H. Pinkham, "Advertising 1875–1953," 6–7.

67. C. H. Pinkham, "Advertising 1875–1953," 7; and Burton, *Lydia Pinkham*, 62–64.

68. C. H. Pinkham, "Advertising 1875–1953," 7.

69. Ibid.; and "Greenback Party," The Free Dictionary, http://www.thefreedictionary.com/Greenback+Party.

70. "Greenback Meeting and Convention," *The Farmers' Cabinet* (Amherst, NH), vol. 77, no. 10, November 10, 1878, 2.

71. C. H. Pinkham, "Advertising 1875–1953," 7; and "Politics and Rum," ca. November 1879, clipping in Lydia E. Pinkham, "Lydia's Scrapbook, 1870's, 1880's," MC 181, vol. 556, frame 81 of 473 scans in the author's possession.

72. Burton, *Lydia Pinkham*, 60–61; and Stage, *Female Complaints*, 28.

73. C. H. Pinkham, "Advertising 1875–1953," 8.

74. Burton, *Lydia Pinkham*, 65–66; and Stage, *Female Complaints*, 27, 30.

75. Burton, *Lydia Pinkham*, 65–66. C. H. Pinkham, "Advertising 1875–1953," 4–5.

76. "The Panic of 1873," History Engine, http://historyengine.richmond.edu/episodes/view/308.

77. Stage, *Female Complaints*, 30.

78. Earle Stern, "Old Recipe Made Lydia Pinkham Household Word," *The Daily Item*, December 24, 1968, 5.

2

Lydia Stands Up, Stands Out

The period from 1837 to 1901 was known as the Victorian Era, so named after Queen Victoria's reign. It was not exactly a shining time for women. Victorian morality, a collection of moral and ethical views transported from the United Kingdom to America, espoused such values as subdued sexuality and a strict social code of conduct.[1] Most women knew their place was not to speak out on social issues nor to achieve a high level of education nor to help the masses deal with medical issues nor to be a part of the entrepreneurial world.

Lydia Pinkham was not most women. She may have shared the same birth year with Queen Victoria, but she was ahead of her time in so many other respects.[2] She did speak out, achieve, advise, and succeed, which set her apart and laid the foundation for her family's future success.

But she did so while also falling in line with some of the expectations of the day. Women's clothes reflected society's value of modesty. Dresses came in several layers so as to be sure to conceal the skin. "Mutton-leg" sleeves added to the concealment. Men dressed conservatively, as well, but women found doing so more difficult because their clothes made it challenging to move around.[3]

Women also had to embody a number of mores and behaviors, such as when walking on the street they were expected to go about their business quietly and never attract others' attention. Should they recognize someone, a gentleman was greeted first with a smile or a bow but never by his first name. A woman's language must never be critical and always should be unassuming. She must not start conflicts and, in general, should be quiet.[4]

Domestic chores were chief among most women's duties. Some aspects of that changed with the advent of industrialization, which allowed such homemade goods as candles, soaps, and clothes to be manufactured more cheaply. Although industrialization created job opportunities, immigrant workers were mostly the ones who took advantage. In 1850, women made up only 13 percent of the paid labor force, with most choosing to work either in agriculture or domestic service instead.[5]

By choosing a domestic role, a woman could more easily achieve the standard of "decency" that maintained a nonworking wife was a symbol of her husband's earning power.[6] With many women confined to their homes, the perception of men as strong and women as weak was commonly held at the time.[7] Nonetheless, those same women faced more than their share of important responsibilities, such as caring for family members when they were ill. Many relied on home remedies, and few were more prepared for this eventuality than Lydia Pinkham. In fact, it was her use of different mixtures to treat various ailments that brought her recognition at the community level, and later it was her development of what became known as the Vegetable Compound that would establish her place in history.

She would go on to play a leadership role in the family enterprise, a rarity in a time when women-run businesses were little more than a slow-growing niche. Although women tycoons of the day could be counted on one hand (not using all the fingers), a few women were finding top jobs in nondurable goods industries or were managing aspects of family-owned endeavors.[8]

Lydia took the latter role to a whole new level. She did so at a time when some of the Victorian conventions were beginning to moderate. For many people, marriage worked well as a permanent state, but the growing awareness of spousal abuse and desertion was leading pragmatic individuals to question whether matrimony was always a pleasant fate.[9] Although many believed women were ill-suited to being educated because that would interfere with their roles as wives and mothers, others saw education's importance as women increasingly assumed discretionary power over family financial resources.[10]

In the realm of entrepreneurship, a woman without training or acumen was at a definite disadvantage. A business book about the period had this to say:

> Women inventors faced particular obstacles made more difficult by their gender. Acquiring patents required elaborate models, scale drawings, and sometimes exorbitant fees to obtain and protect exclusive rights to inventions. The technical skills and high costs associated with patent applications presented challenges to women . . . whose work experiences provided them with ideas for improved production processes but not necessarily the funds or legal knowledge to protect their inventions.[11]

Considering these challenges, Lydia's ability to apply her medicinal skills and achieve success with the Vegetable Compound stands as an impressive achievement.

By engaging in more aspects of business, Lydia and those who followed her example helped redefine the aspirations and expectations of future generations of women. Change has come to some professions, but women's inroads elsewhere have been less visible. Despite progress in such fields as law and medicine, all too often such jobs as teacher and nurse have worn the brand "women's professions."[12]

In the nineteenth century, the medical community's exclusion of women not only robbed them of opportunities but engendered a system that too often ignored female ailments and neglected the female body. Although this closed the door on many women, it opened the door for Lydia Pinkham.

NOTES

1. Sally Mitchell, *Daily Life in Victorian England* (Westport, CT: Greenwood Press, 1996) xiii–xv; and Lorence Hartley, *The Ladies' Book of Etiquette and Manual of Politeness* (Boston: Lee & Shepard, Publishers, 1872), passim.

2. "Victoria (r. 1837–1901), *The Official Website of the British Monarchy*, http://www.royal.gov.uk/historyofthemonarchy/kingsandqueensoftheunitedkingdom/thehanoverians/victoria.aspx; and *Pinkham Pioneers* (Lynn, MA: Lydia E. Pinkham Medicine Company, 1927), 2, MC 181 2456, no. 137, The Lydia E. Pinkham Medicine Company Records, Schlesinger Library, Radcliffe Institute, Harvard University.

3. Hartley, *The Ladies' Book of Etiquette*, 21–33.

4. Ibid., passim.

5. Sarah Stage, *Female Complaints: Lydia Pinkham and the Business of Women's Medicine* (New York: Norton, 1979), 65; and Lydia Kingsmill Commander, *The American Idea* (New York: Barnes, 1907), 192.

6. Thorstein Veblen, *The Theory of the Leisure Class* (New York: Macmillan, 1899; repr., Oxford, UK: Oxford University Press, 2007), 42–43; and Jean Burton, *Lydia Pinkham Is Her Name* (New York: Little and Ives, 1949), 66.

7. Charlotte Perkins Gilman, *Women and Economics* (Boston: Small, Maynard, 1898), 4–5; and Stage, *Female Complaints*, 67.

8. Angel Kwolek-Folland, *Incorporating Women: A History of Women and Business in the United States* (New York: Twayne, 1998), 57, 59.

9. Ibid., 68.

10. Ibid., 70.

11. Ibid., 73.

12. Ibid., 127–28.

3

Of Bloodletting and Poisons

The world Lydia was about to enter could be described in four words: *dangerous, archaic, unscrupulous,* and *alienating.* And those were not its worst features. That's because women's medical treatment, as practiced in the nineteenth century, was also often barbaric, horrific, and misogynist. It was a realm populated by bloodsuckers, poisons, and addictive drugs, opium and cocaine chief among them. There were victims not patients, sickness not health.

Into this breach came Lydia Pinkham, a woman who would actually listen to women about their ailments. Short on medical training but big of heart, she stood in contrast to doctors content to rely on an assortment of leeches and scalpels to do their bloodletting, often with little concern for outcomes. In her arsenal were traditional remedies based on herbs and other organic ingredients. But perhaps Lydia's most effective weapon in combatting the medical quackery of the day was her capacity to listen. By applying what she knew about women and their bodies, Lydia could help them fight their way past one misdiagnosis after another to a place of hope. Her Vegetable Compound, with its curious blend of alcohol and unicorn root, was by no means a wonder drug, but as an alternative to the more nefarious options available to women, it often worked wonders.

In pre– and post–Civil War America, many doctors employed such techniques as blistering and cupping to rid patients of various ailments. Medicines for internal use included "nux vomica" (made from a deciduous tree that is a key source of various poisons), "vermifuges" (which expelled intestinal worms), quinine, calomel, and antimony. Calomel was a white salt mixture of mercury and chloride once used as an insecticide. It left a burning pain in the throat, bowels, and stomach, causing vomiting and painful cramps.[1] Patients who didn't feel better after taking an ounce of calomel were directed to take more.[2] If consumed repeatedly, the buildup of mercury could lead to toxic aftereffects, such as extreme salivation, rotting teeth, gangrene, and reduced heart activity.³

Like calomel, cocaine gained widespread acceptance as a cure-all drug. Before its physical and psychological effects became known, cocaine was thought to have health benefits and was considered a fitness tonic that could be found (in small amounts) in such soft drinks as Coca-Cola. Some physicians would self-medicate with cocaine, leading to their downfalls.⁴

Women who had been adversely affected by calomel wrote to Lydia seeking advice. One described her ailment:

> It is an affection of the gums and the mucous membrane of the mouth—the gums turn white and a layer easily rubs off leaving them very red and angry, . . . the inside of my cheeks and corners of my jaw are white and look and feel hot and parboiled and contracted, it had extended to my tonsils and seems to have started down my throat. . . . I have also womb trouble, constant pain in the small of the back. . . . I have [an] enlarged urethra, the mouth is wide open all the time large enough to admit a small bean, sometimes it gives me great trouble and agony and is then comfortable for a time. I sleep well and my appetite is good, and I am regular in my bowels, but not strong, no endurance.⁵

Lydia answered, "You have taken virulent poisons in the form of [medicines] that have caused disease of the mucous membranes." Without examining the woman, Lydia decided she had mercurial poisoning.⁶

Nineteenth-century medicine could be summed up with this phrase from a prominent physician—"ineffectual speculation." Cures were sometimes created for ailments about which physicians knew nothing. The public pressured doctors to make changes and produce results, leading many practitioners to resort to extreme procedures, which in turn struck fear into the populace.⁷ There to comfort the terrified women were Lydia and a small army of patent medicine sellers, most diligent, others not so much.

It is little wonder that the masses turned to them. Patient deaths often were treated casually by the medical establishment. Dr. Benjamin Rush (1745–1813), a prominent Philadelphian physician and signer of the Declaration of Independence, told his students at the University of Pennsylvania, "The death of a patient, under the ill-directed operations of nature, or what are called lenient and safe medicines, seldom injures the reputation or business of a physician. For this reason many people are permitted to die who might have been recovered through the use of efficient remedies."⁸

Many also were cavalier about their treatments. In bloodletting, physicians sometimes would take so much fluid from patients that they would faint. The amount of blood drawn from a patient highly varied depending on the ailment and the physician. Some of the sick were bled for only 6 ounces while Dr. Rush stated that his friend had 90 ounces of blood drawn in a single sitting. Considering that the average 150-pound human has a little over 160 ounces of blood, the quantities drawn were quite alarming. If that technique didn't relieve, say, a menstruation issue, leeches often were applied directly on a woman's cervix.⁹ Some doctors bragged about their histories, with one writer relating, "He verily believed he had drawn more than one hundred barrels of blood during his medical career and had yet to see the first instance in which he had drawn blood to the injury of the patient."[10]

In earlier centuries, bloodletting had been considered so cruel that the Catholic Church instituted a rule in 1163 prohibiting monks and priests from practicing it. So the role shifted to barbers, with lore holding that the poles outside their establishments evolved from the red symbolizing blood, the white representing bandages and the blue ball on top signifying the leech basin.[11]

Blistering was similarly suspect. By raising a blister using cantharides or tartar emetic plasters and then separating the wound and expelling the pus, physicians contended that infections were drawn out of the body. This remedy obviously did more harm than good.[12]

By some physicians' own admissions, ailments in many instances would have gone away on their own. Dr. Richard C. Cabot, a medical professor at Harvard University, once said, "Three-quarters of all illnesses are cured without the victims even knowing they have had them." With *victim* being an interesting choice of word, Cabot further asserted,

> Proof of this contention is to be found in post-mortem examinations, which time after time reveal indelible and unmistakable traces of disease which the subject has conquered, all unknowingly. Ninety per cent of all typhoid cures itself, as does 75 per cent of all pneumonia. In fact, out of a total of 215 diseases known to medical science, there are only about eight or nine which doctors conquer—the rest conquer themselves.[13]

Even though plenty of ailments were cured simply with time, many patients were led to believe that the treatments they were receiving helped speed their return to health.

Eventually, though, patients' skepticism began to grow, which, combined with the fact that doctors remained an economic luxury to most of the public, led many people to rely on home remedies and self-treatments.[14] These twin issues would hinder one approach to medical treatment while giving rise to another.

In a way, the physicians' worst enemy was the fee structure of the day. Most patients paid on a per-service or per-case basis, while others relied on a fixed fee, which meant if a case lingered, the doctor wouldn't see any additional income.[15] Either way, most medical care was performed on credit. Because doctors typically collected fees quarterly or annually, they often had little income (five hundred dollars annually) and many unpaid bills. Although some became wealthy, the majority struggled to make a decent living.[16]

Frustrated with physicians' remedies, some individuals took matters into their own hands. Farmer Samuel Thomson created a botanical medicine system that gave men and women the ability to cure their ailments. Thomson lost faith in doctors when they failed to save his mother, asserting that they "gave her disease the name of galloping consumption, which I thought was a very appropriate name—for they are the riders, and their whip is mercury, opium and vitriol, and they galloped her out of the world in about nine weeks."[17]

In Thomson's simplified view of his medical system, "Heat is life, Cold is death," with the stomach acting like the body's furnace. Because disease festered in the stomach, the cure was to cleanse it and the bowels. Thomson's therapy did so by raising the body's external heat to induce a sweat, then using the herb lobelia for cleansing and employing cayenne to raise internal heat. Later, vegetable tonics were used to strengthen the stomach and restore digestion.[18]

The medical community ridiculed Thomson, labeling him the "puke doctor." In 1809, he was brought to trial for allegedly killing three patients with lobelia. When he was unexpectedly acquitted, his popularity spread, and in retaliation, the medical establishment championed legislation to block his system. The embattled Thomson sought government protection, and in 1813, a patent protected his treatment program, which individuals could purchase for twenty dollars so long as they agreed to protect its secrets.[19]

Thomson's botanical movement flourished though the 1830s in New England, parts of New York, and the South. Women, in particular, liked the idea of educating themselves about their ailments. Thomson died in 1843, claiming more than three million followers and perhaps smoothing the way for Lydia Pinkham's Vegetable Compound.[20] Although some of his techniques did women little good, he showed there were credible alternatives to accepted medical practices.

For women, having access to more humane medical treatment was only half the battle. They wanted to be able to talk freely about their "women's problems," discuss their children's health issues, and feel comfortable doing so.

Too often prudishness on the one hand and uncaring male doctors on the other led to mistaken diagnoses. In writing to Lydia, they gained the confidence to open up in ways that only a woman-to-woman dialogue could provide. The following letter about a woman's reluctance to see renowned Philadelphia physician Charles Meigs in 1838 illustrates the oversized role modesty sometimes played:

> I cannot give any further information beyond what you could yourself obtain from Mrs.—. As the wife of a medical man, she is aware that false delicacy too often injures females, by their allowing disease to get beyond the reach of medical art before they speak out. I have told her to answer any question you should think necessary to ask her.[21]

But that was hardly the only obstacle they faced. French historian Jules Michelet's widely read book *L'Amour* called the rising interest in women's health issues the great malady of the nineteenth century, characterizing the period as the "age of the womb."[22] He likened the concern to leprosy, which plagued the thirteenth century, and to syphilis, which tormented the sixteenth. He wasn't done. Writing about menstruation, he said, "So that, in reality, 15 or 20 days out of 28 (we may say nearly always) woman is not only invalid, but a wounded one. She ceaselessly suffers from love's eternal wound."[23]

When it came to assessing their suitability for the medical profession, women also got no love from Harvard professor Cabot, a leading intellectual and a member of one of America's most prominent families. Considering women's "limitations" in mind, body, and spirit, he said they should be relegated to activities that demanded less intellectual acumen. He added that the best a woman could hope for was to try "medical social work" because a regular practice was "too competitive and warlike."[24]

For women, it got even worse. Even their sex organs were cause for discrimination. Many of the more reverent folks from the era considered the reproductive system to be the central part of a woman. In this sacred trust, the uterus had to be protected in the interest of the human race, leading one doctor to proclaim, "The Almighty, in creating the female sex, had taken the uterus and built up a woman around it."[25] With a woman thus diminished, misconceptions multiplied and poor treatments often followed. Lydia was left to proclaim, "Only a woman can understand a woman's ills."

Dr. Meigs, considered one of the most distinguished medical men of his day, added to women's plight. In his textbook on obstetrics, female patients were referred to as the "dear little ladies" with heads "almost too small for intellect but just big enough for love."[26]

Even progressive thinkers of the time wouldn't cut women a break. Lydia's contemporary Nathan Davis, a public health advocate who would go on to help found the American Medical Association (AMA), was opposed to women entering the medical field. Although he told colleagues that separate medical schools for women might be "tolerated," he was opposed to coed institutions and did not support the right for women to become AMA members.[27]

Although Lydia was never at the forefront of the medical school debate, other women of her time began pushing for change as early as the 1840s. Those who petitioned for admittance met stark opposition, including Elizabeth Blackwell, who in 1849 became the first female to earn a medical degree.[28] But for that step forward, there was another step back the very next year when Dr. Oliver Wendell Holmes (a well-known physician and writer of his day) tried to admit a female student to the Harvard Medical School. The student body quickly overruled him, summing up the sentiments of this time period: "Resolved that we are not opposed to allowing woman her rights, but we do protest against her appearing in places where her presence is calculated to destroy our respect for the modesty and delicacy of her sex."[29]

Similarly, years later, even though seventeen medical colleges had been established for women in the United States, females still struggled to be admitted to the elite medical schools. In the early 1890s, when prestigious Johns Hopkins needed more funding, it agreed to admit women but only in return for a $500,000 endowment from a group of wealthy women.[30]

Despite these challenges, there were some victories along the way. Advances in preventative medicine became one of women's major contributions to the health field. Blackwell and her physician sister gained prominence by opening a medical school in New York, where they introduced a course in hygiene that led to better health practices.[31] Lydia had a role in this endeavor by contributing to better habits through her health guides and her correspondence with women.

As practiced in the nineteenth century, gynecology was crude to the point of being demeaning. Before things got better, a combination of false modesty and male authority meant exams were performed with the female patient fully dressed and the doctor kneeling before her with his hands up her skirt, his eyes averted. Because the physician could touch but not expose the genitalia, clinical thoroughness was lacking and misdiagnosis rampant.[32] Contemporary writer Catharine Beecher worried aloud that doctors would take advantage of patients, while suffragist Mary Livermore labeled physicians an "unclean army of gynecologists."[33]

The practice improved as women's health issues came slowly to the fore. J. Marion Sims was renowned for his work and received the title "father of American gynecology." Other advances followed, although specialists were scorned by many in the medical community, with some doubting whether women would ever go to them in large numbers. Dr. Meigs, in his book *Females and Their Diseases*, published in 1848, stated, "I am proud to say . . . that there are women who prefer to suffer the extremity of danger and pain rather than waive those scruples of delicacy which prevent their maladies from being fully explored."[34]

Despite the ridicule, gynecologists often corrected such problems as vaginal discharge that either had been neglected by physicians or made worse under their care. In the case of a prolapsed uterus, a condition that involved the weakening of ligaments that support the organ, the prevailing treatment often was surgery. Doctors misdiagnosed the causes as dancing, singing, skating, and horseback riding, when the source generally was repeated pregnancies or harsh physical labor. Surgery usually was not required.[35] Lydia, who rarely met the women who wrote to her about such matters, prided herself on making the correct original diagnosis and treatment. She would encourage women not to let their modesty prevent them from describing their symptoms.[36]

Surgery practices also improved as anesthesia (through chloroform) came into general use in 1843. Ether also became a practical anesthetic about the same time as the then-more-popular chloroform in the 1840s. The first public demonstration of controlled administration of ether took place on October 16, 1846, at Massachusetts General Hospital, under the direction of a dentist and Harvard medical student, William T. G. Morton (Morton left Harvard before completing his program), but Dr. J. C. Warren performed the actual surgery, surrounded by other Harvard medical professors. A glass globe type inhaler was used to administer the ether to the patient by means of a wooden or glass mouthpiece tube.[37] Although some religious groups for years argued against its use in childbirth, anesthesia helped the gynecological field rise to prominence.[38] But not everyone favored more surgeries, especially to remove ovaries, a procedure with a mortality rate as high as 40 percent.[39] Because no amount of assurance could ease the terror many women felt, ads for Lydia's Vegetable Compound promoted the medicine as an alternative to surgery.

Despite advances and women's steady march into the medical field, their numbers in the professions began to decrease around the turn of the century. Only 3 women's medical schools existed in 1909, down from 17, and the total number of female medical students, including those enrolled at coed schools, decreased from 1,419 (15 years earlier) to 921. Opposition to their presence persisted from males and administrators. Some schools attempted to limit the number of women accepted into medical programs. Disregarding wartime, quotas capped female enrollment at 5 percent after 1910, a practice that lasted for almost half a century.[40]

Through all the expansions and contractions, through all of the advancements and setbacks, one thing held steady: Lydia's belief in herself and her remedies meant that she was about to bring her Vegetable Compound to the public, and with that, the world of medicine would never be the same.

NOTES

1. Dorry Baird Norris, *Lydia Pinkham: Herbal Entrepreneur* (Franklin, TN: Sage Cottage, 1996), 2.

2. Jennifer Schmid, "Beautiful Black Poison: The History of Calomel as Medicine in America," *The Weston A. Price Foundation*, April 2, 2009, http://www.westonaprice.org/; and Jean Burton, *Lydia Pinkham Is Her Name* (New York: Little and Ives, 1949), 46.

3. Ira Rutkow, *Seeking the Cure* (New York: Scribner, 2010), 38.

4. Ibid., 128; and Peter Olch, "William S. Halsted and Local Anesthesia: Contributions and Complications," *Anesthesiology* 42 (1975): 483.

5. Lydia E. Pinkham, "Medical Directions for Ailments," ca. 1878, vol. 537, 58–60, The Lydia E. Pinkham Medicine Company Records, Schlesinger Library, Radcliffe Institute, Harvard University.

6. Ibid.

7. Jacob Bigelow, "On Self Limited Diseases," paper presented before the Massachusetts Medical Society, May 27, 1835, reprinted in Gert H. Brieger (ed.), *Medical America in the Nineteenth Century: Readings from the Literature* (Baltimore: Johns Hopkins Press, 1972), 99; and Sarah Stage, *Female Complaints: Lydia Pinkham and the Business of Women's Medicine* (New York: Norton, 1979), 47.

8. Benjamin Rush, *Six Introductory Lectures, to Courses of Lectures, upon the Institutes and Practices of Medicine, Delivered in the University of Pennsylvania* (Philadelphia: Conrad, 1801), 69, cited in Stage, *Female Complaints*.

9. James Henry Bennet, *Inflammation of the Uterus*, 3rd ed. (London: John Churchill, 1853), 266–67; Clutterbuck, "Proper Administration of Blood-Letting for the Prevention and Cure of Disease," (London: S. Highley, 1840), 30–31; and "Blood, How Much Do We Have?" MedicineNet.com, http://www.medicinenet.com/script/main/art.asp?articlekey=21474; "Bloodletting Is Back! Here's Everything You Need to Know about This Ancient Practice," *Medtech*, http://www.medtech.edu/blog/the-history-progression-and-modern-stance-on-bloodletting.

10. Rutkow, *Seeking the Cure*, 38.

11. "Patients' Voices in Early 19th Century Virginia," *University of Virginia*, http://carmichael.lib.virginia.edu/story/tools.html; "Bloodletting Is Back!"; and Gwen Bruno, "Why Was There Bloodletting in Barber Shops?" *eHow*, http://www.ehow.com/facts_5719000_there-bloodletting-barber-shops_.html.

12. William G. Rothstein, *American Physicians in the Nineteenth Century* (Baltimore: Johns Hopkins Press, 1972), 53, cited in Stage, *Female Complaints*.

13. Robert Collier, *The Secret of the Ages* (Originally published: New York: Robert Collier, 1926; and Global Grey edition, e-book, 2013), 198.

14. Stage, *Female Complaints*, 50.

15. Paul Starr, *The Social Transformation of American Medicine* (New York: Basic Books, 1982), 63.

16. Ibid.; and Barnes Riznik, "Medicine in New England, 1790–1840" (Old Sturbridge Village, MA: unpublished manuscript, 1963), 78–81.

17. Samuel Thomson, *Narrative of the Life and Medical Discoveries of Samuel Thomson*, 5th ed. (St. Clairsville, OH: Horton Howard, 1829), 14.

18. Samuel Thomson, *New Guide to Health*, 2nd ed. (Boston: J. Q. Adams, 1835), 18; John A. Brown, *The Family Guide to Health* (Providence, RI: B. T. Albro, 1837), 39–40, digitized by Open Knowledge Commons, U.S. National Library of Medicine; and Stage, *Female Complaints*, 53.

19. Samuel Thomson, *Report of the Trial of Dr. Samuel Thomson* (Boston: Author, 1839); John Thomson, *A Vindication of the Thomsonian System* (Albany, NY: Webster and Wood, 1825), 42–43; Thomson, *Narrative*, 117–22, 162–72; and Stage, *Female Complaints*, 53.

20. Stage, *Female Complaints*, 54; and Thomson, *Report*, 51.

21. Richard Harrison Shryock, *Medicine and Society in America, 1660–1860* (New York: University Press, 1960), 120–21.

22. Stage, *Female Complaints*, 64; and Jules Michelet, *L'Amour*, 4th Paris ed., trans. J. W. Palmer (New York: Carleton, 1868), 1*.

23. Michelet, *L'Amour*, 48, cited in Stage, *Female Complaints*.

24. Eugene Perry Link, *The Social Ideas of American Physicians* (London: Associated University Presses, 1992), 205.

25. Frederick Hollick, *The Origin of Life and the Process of Reproduction* (New York: American News, 1878), 683; and Carroll Smith-Rosenberg and Charles Rosenberg, "The Female Animal: Medical and Biological Views of Woman and Her Role in Nineteenth-Century America," *Journal of American History* 60, no. 2 (September 1973): 335, cited in Stage, *Female Complaints*.

26. Shryock, *Medicine and Society*, 121; and Charles D. Meigs, *Females and Their Diseases* (Philadelphia: Lea and Blanchard, 1848), 47.

27. Link, *Social Ideas*, 81.

28. Ibid., 96–97; and "Elizabeth Blackwell," Bio, http://www.biography.com/people/elizabeth-blackwell-9214198.

29. Burton, *Lydia Pinkham*, 40; and Link, *Social Ideas*, 39.

30. Mary R. Walsh, *"Doctors Wanted, No Women Need Apply": Sexual Barriers in the Medical Profession, 1835–1975* (New Haven, CT: Yale University Press, 1978), 176–77, 192.

31. Link, *Social Ideas*, 151.

32. Stage, *Female Complaints*, 78; and [Ettore] Ciuli, "Storia generale dell' esplorazione," illustration in J. P. (Jacques Pierre) Maygrier, *Nuove Dimostrazioni di Ostetricia* (Pisa: Nistri, 1831), illustration 29.

33. Catharine E. Beecher, *Letters to the People on Health and Happiness* (New York: Harper, 1855), 135; and Mary A. Livermore, introductory letter to George Lowell Austin, *Perils of American Women* (Boston: Lee and Shepard, 1883), cited in Stage, *Female Complaints*.

34. Meigs, *Females and Their Diseases*, 19, cited in Stage, *Female Complaints*.

35. Austin, *Perils of American Women*, 163–81; Albert Hamilton Hayes, *Sexual Physiology of Woman, and Her Diseases; or Woman, Treated Physiologically, Pathologically, and Esthetically* (Boston: Peabody Medical Institute, 1869), 316; and Stage, *Female Complaints*, 78–79.

36. "I Hate to Ask My Doctor," *Advertisements in Periodicals*, vol. 1, *1890–1900*, The Lydia E. Pinkham Medicine Company Records, Schlesinger Library, Radcliffe Institute, Harvard University.

37. Jessica B. Murphy, reference archivist, Center for the History of Medicine, Francis A. Countway Library of Medicine, Harvard Medical School; "Ether and Chloroform," *History.com*, 2010, http://www.history.com/topics/ether-and-chloroform; "Ether Inhaler, ca. 1840's," *Countway Repository*, http://repository.countway.harvard.edu/xmlui/handle/10473/1785. Also note the following paintings for examples of the first ether administrations: Robert Hinckley, *First Operation under Ether*, painted from 1882–1894; and Warren and Lucia Prosperi, *Ether Dome Painting*, 2000, http://www.massgeneral.org/history/exhibits/ether-dome-painting.

38. Robert B. Hoffman and Donald E. Martin, "The History of Modern Anesthesia," *Pennsylvania Society of Anesthesiologists*, http://www.psanes.org/Home/tabid/37/anid/43/Default.aspx.

39. Edwin M. Jameson, *Gynecology and Obstetrics* (New York: Hoeber, 1936), 128, cited in Stage, *Female Complaints*.

40. Starr, *Social Transformation*, 124.

4

Of Patent Medicines, Abuses and All

Talk about the ultimate sleight of hand. Imagine an enterprise built on promises of comfort and relief that in reality delivered false hopes and little else. Now, imagine that this undertaking raked in tens of millions dollars in an era when a million actually meant something, and you have a snapshot of the patent medicine trade of the late nineteenth century.

Kidney trouble? "We've got the cure for what ails you," the traveling pitchmen would tell small-town believers. Whooping cough? With this product, your troubles are over, the newspaper ad would shout to thousands more. Lofty claims indeed, no matter their truths. For in the 1870s, and even one hundred years before that, the proof wasn't in the healing but in the dealing. From traveling medicine shows to testimonials to enormous images that defaced the sides of barns, few techniques were left untried, and few embellishments were left unsaid.

Patent medicines are typically associated with eighteenth- and nineteenth-century drug compounds sold to the public bearing lofty claims and bold names. While a drug may be labeled as a patent medicine, in actuality most of the nineteenth-century concoctions were never officially patented. Rather, the majority of remedies were only trademarked and could easily be purchased without a prescription.[1]

Even Lydia Pinkham, who once in the business generally stayed above such flim-flam in promotions yet still stretched credibility with some of her claims, would feel obliged at times to rely on a doctor's endorsement to legitimize her products, despite her oft-trumpeted aversion to surgeons. So, it's little wonder that this barrage of pitches from the patent medicine industry convinced Americans to part with their hard-earned dollars, conveying riches to the purveyors. Such critics as Harvard's Dr. Holmes labeled the latter "toadstool millionaires" because of what he said were fortunes founded on fabrication, deception, and conceit.[2]

The buy-this-remedy pattern took hold in this country at the dawn of America's independence from Britain. In 1774, John Boyd's "medicinal store" advertised the powers of medicines imported from London. In fact, in the half century prior, colonists on this side of the Atlantic had developed a dependence on English drugs. That obsession went unfulfilled when the Revolutionary War disrupted trade between the two countries, and into the vacuum stepped counterfeiters who filled old bottles of English medicines with creations of their own. Once the war ended, foreign brands returned to these shores, but the impersonators were taking their place with the public.[3]

As Americans purchased homegrown medicines with pride, products made in the United States began to flourish and even make their way back to England.[4] The first American to patent a medicine was Samuel Lee Jr., whose Bilious Pills cured everything from yellow fever to dysentery and female complaints.[5]

Other ambitious drug proprietors began placing column-long advertisements in newspapers nationwide, with the promotions eventually accounting for one-third of all advertising profits.[6] Distinctively named products emerged, including Hamilton's Grand Restorative.[7] Early on, bottle shapes and not ingredients were patent protected. Copyrights at the time lasted for twenty-eight years and could be renewed for fourteen more, covering label images and text.[8] Dr. Holmes and other critics argued that patent medicines weren't worthy of protection because they were prescribed to fight off diseases that didn't exist by "doctors" who weren't really physicians and backed by statistical evidence that in reality didn't support their claims.[9]

When Lydia decided to enter the world of patent medicines in 1875, she generally steered clear of such tactics, adopting strategies that set her apart. She didn't need to fabricate testimonials because women by the hundreds were writing her for advice, so many that she one day would have to hire folks to reply to them in her name. Her company even put $5,000 in escrow to guarantee their authenticity. She didn't go down the road of conjuring up illnesses, but her ads weren't shy about implying that the compound could soothe various life-threatening symptoms. Lydia never pretended to be a doctor, instead asserting she knew more about women's ailments than most doctors. She relied on anecdotal rather than statistical evidence to back her claims.[10]

Even though Lydia would adhere to at least some standards, not many other practitioners did. When making a pitch, no topic was taboo, no stage too grand, no name untouchable. Public figures from President Lincoln on down were fodder for promotional copy, such as this advertisement on the front page of the *New York Herald*:

President Lincoln (repeated three times)
Did you see him? (repeated four times)
Did you see his whiskers? (three times)
Raised in six weeks by the use of (only once)
Bellingham's [ointment] (six times)[11]

It was during the Civil War that patent medicines started to come into their own. While fighting claimed many lives over the course of the war, disease was the main culprit. Soldiers stricken with an ailment did not have much to turn to. Alcohol would have been used to numb the pain, but liquor rations had been prohibited by the army in 1832. As an alternative, the high alcohol content in patent medicines became a suitable substitute. Civilians also started turning to patent medicines for their alcohol content because, unlike liquor, patent medicines weren't taxed. Thus from after the Civil War in 1865, the heyday of patent medicine began, which would last roughly until 1906 with the passage of the Pure Food and Drug Act.[12]

Newspapers, long the vehicle for helping patent medicine merchants spread their word, had become even more attractive when readers grew hungry for news about the Civil War. Expanded daily issues and new Sunday editions created more advertising opportunities, even as publishers sought cheaper ways to print. Cotton rag newsprint at twenty-four cents a pound was used until about the 1870s, when less-expensive wood pulp paper replaced it. Although the newspaper–patent medicine partnership would thrive for years to come, at times gulping up 90 percent of the Pinkhams' annual ad budget along the way, many other promotional ploys would be tried, from the bold to the subtle.[13]

Building from a valuation of $3.5 million in 1859 to $74.5 million by 1904, the patent medicine juggernaut was becoming a social and economic force with few boundaries.[14] Critics charged it crossed the line with "scare tactic" ads that would drum fear into the minds of consumers by exaggerating minor irregularities, such as back pain, into the symptoms for kidney disease. Those fears often equated to more sales, as did pitches made during disease outbreaks that became epidemics.[15]

Other techniques relied on appeals to patriotism, if not good taste, such as an ad featuring Uncle Sam sitting at a table, document in hand, with the caption, "This is to certify that I am using 100,000 boxes of Ex-Lax every month." Religion and ministers also were not off limits, as with this ad: "By eating a bowl of Grape-Nuts after my Sabbath work is done my nerves are quieted and rest and refreshing sleep are ensured me."[16]

Already accounting for 25 percent of all newspaper advertising, patent medicine advertising popped up everywhere, from posters to fences.[17] This led some critics to bunch the industry with others they blamed for the "Age of Disfigurement." In complaining that beautiful scenery in the mid-1870s was being compromised for advertising purposes, an editorialist for the *New-York Tribune* mused,

> There is an ancient nuisance now bursting into a development so glaring that it calls for a universal protest. . . . It is not enough that fences and sheds are painted over with the names of nostrums; enormous signs are erected in the fields, not a rock is left without disfigurement. . . . The agents of these nostrums range the whole country, painting rocks, fences, and sheds in violation of the owner's will—oftentimes by night—and disposing in the same manner of the bridges belonging to counties and municipalities. They take special pains to visit all places of summer resort, violating the beauty of mountain scenery, and the seclusion of the remotest valleys. They have long since

crossed the continent, and laid their unclean paws on the Rocky Mountains and the Sierra Nevada.[18]

Author and English traveler W. G. Marshall was similarly moved to say that advertisements are "one of the first things that strike the stranger as soon as he has landed in the New World; he cannot step a mile into the open country, whether into the fields or along the high roads, without meeting the disfigurement. . . . The nuisance culminates at Chicago, for here is the paradise of 'white-paintism.'"[19] In travel essays, fellow author Robert Louis Stevenson also was discouraged by the amount of advertising he saw in America.[20]

Patent medicine's influence was growing at the expense of traditional medical professions, challenging the authority of pharmacists and doctors. A writer in *Druggist Circular* had this complaint about many pharmacists' practice of promoting competitors, such as, say, the Lydia Pinkham Company, which years later would mail out 10,000 portraits of Lydia at druggists' requests[21]

> How stupid can pharmacists be? . . . They give away valuable window display space to show goods which are making their sworn enemies rich; they hang pictures and tack signs of their biggest rivals in the most conspicuous place in their stores; they plaster their windows with transparencies and give place on the sidewalk to all kinds of signs and bicycle racks, to the end that a quack living in a distant city, a doctor who is too sick to practice, or a "retired missionary" who is too strong to work, may wax opulent.[22]

The upstart rival was not content with traditional advertising techniques, sometimes going to extremes to deliver its message. One such stunt was the traveling medicine show, featuring actors, bigger-than-life exploits, and other forms of entertainment in mostly small-town venues. Pitches alternated with magic tricks, comedy, and expert marksmanship feats. A typical scare tactic might warn, "You laughing, happy audience; you mother; you father; you young man, woman, and child, every one of you—within you are seeds of death! Is it cancer? Is it consumption? Is it perhaps some unknown malady?"[23] Some shows included vaudeville acts and burlesque, drawing thousands in Chicago, New York, and Boston.[24] With a solid, professional performance, according to *Advertising World*, a pitchman could sell "more goods in half an hour than [the legitimate storekeeper] sells in a month. The street vendor comes to town, opens up his pack, spends half an hour 'advertising' his stock orally, aided with a few sleight-of-hand tricks . . . or a little slow music, and then proceeds to sell to your customers the very same goods you have had in your store for a month or more."[25] To add an air of legitimacy, doctors sometimes backed a pitchman's claims, although most had lost their practices through either incompetence or alcohol abuse.[26]

Physicians and pharmacists responded to the patent medicine challenge in different ways. Traditionally, consumers would seek medicine for ailments from an unlicensed pharmacist without a prescription.[27] In dispensing medicines, which often were created from scratch, many druggists would either rely on their experiences or acquire their knowledge from the most recent edition of the *American Pharmacopeia*.[28]

Over the years, druggists spent less time mixing medicines, choosing instead to sell premade patent medicines. Grocery and department stores could buy patent medicines in bulk and then sell them at reduced prices to lure customers, almost always undercutting druggists.[29] To compete, pharmacists banded together and cut their prices, forcing some grocery drug sections out of business.[30] A few pharmacists also found a way to make their own drugs again at a profit, leading to conflicts with doctors over prescription safety.[31]

As the medical establishment struggled to respond, the patent medicine industry not only managed to turn huge profits but, in the eyes of advertising historians, also was establishing the country's first brand-name consumer goods. As the twentieth century dawned, Americans were spending $75 million a year on 28,000 types of patent medicines, or about $2.1 billion in 2014 (adjusted for inflation).[32]

The industry's innovative advertising campaigns laid the groundwork for many products to come, including the compound that would make Lydia Pinkham one of the earliest and most recognizable celebrities in America.[33]

NOTES

1. "History of Patent Medicine," *Hagley Museum and Library*, http://www.hagley.org/on-line_exhibits/patentmed/history/history.html; and "Patent Medicine," *Dictionary.com*, http://dictionary.reference.com/browse/patent+medicine.

2. Oliver Wendell Holmes, *Medical Essays 1842–1882* (Boston: Houghton, Mifflin, 1892), 186.

3. James Harvey Young, *The Toadstool Millionaires: A Social History of Patent Medicines in America before Federal Regulation* (Princeton, NJ: Princeton University Press, 1961), 14–15; "Turlington's Original Balsam of Life," *The New-York Mercury*, November 9, 1761, 8; John Wesley, *Primitive Physic: Or, an Easy and Natural Method of Curing Most Diseases*, 24th ed., ed. William M. Cornell (London: J. Paramore, 1785; Boston: Cyrus Stone, 1858), 143–144; and Joseph D. Weeks, "Reports on the Manufacture of Glass," *Report on the Manufactures of the United States at the Tenth Census* (Washington, DC, 1883), 81–82.

4. Young, *Toadstool Millionaires*, 20–21; *New York Journal*, September 5, 1771; and Whitfield J. Bell Jr., "Suggestions for Research in the Local History of Medicine in the United States," *Bulletin of the History of Medicine* 17 (1945): 465.

5. Young, *Toadstool Millionaires*, 32–33.

6. Ann Anderson, *Snake Oil, Hustlers, and Hambones: The American Medicine Show* (Jefferson, NC: McFarland, 2000), 38–41; and Peter Conrad and Valerie Leiter, "From Lydia Pinkham to Queen Levitra: Direct-to-Consumer Advertising and Medicalisation," *Sociology of Health and Illness* 30, no. 6 (2008): 827.

7. Young, *Toadstool Millionaires*, 34.

8. Richard R. Bowker, *Copyright, Its History and Its Law* (Boston, 1912), 36; and Young, *Toadstool Millionaires*, 40.

9. Ibid., 67–68; and Holmes, *Medical Essays*, 186.

10. "I Followed Mrs. Pinkham's Advice and Now I Am Well," *Advertisements in Periodicals*, vol. 1, *1890–1900*, The Lydia E. Pinkham Medicine Company Records, Schlesinger Library, Radcliffe Institute, Harvard University; and Sarah Stage, *Female Complaints: Lydia Pinkham and the Business of Women's Medicine* (New York: Norton, 1979), 153.

11. "Lincoln Ad," *New York Herald*, February 26, 1861, 1.

12. Anderson, *Snake Oil*, 37.

13. Young, *Toadstool Millionaires*, 100; and Thomas D. Clark, *Southern Country Editor* (Indianapolis: Bobbs-Merrill, 1948), 66–71.

14. Young, *Toadstool Millionaires*, 110.

15. Arthur J. Cramp, *Nostrums and Quackery* (Chicago: American Medical Association, 1921), 2:802–3; and Arthur J. Cramp, *Nostrums and Quackery* (Chicago: American Medical Association, 1936), 3:120, cited in Young, *Toadstool Millionaires*.

16. Young, *Toadstool Millionaires*, 185.

17. Anderson, *Snake Oil*, 38–41; and Conrad and Leiter, "From Lydia Pinkham," 827.

18. Young, *Toadstool Millionaires*, 120; Arthur P. Kimball, "The Age of Disfigurement," *Outlook* 57 (October 30, 1897): 521–24; and "An Intolerable Nuisance," *New-York Tribune*, May 13, 1876, 4, col. 4.

19. Marcus Dickey, *The Youth of James Whitcomb Riley* (Indianapolis: Bobbs-Merrill, 1919), 105–14, 137; W. G. Marshall, *Through America* (London: Sampson Low, Marston, Searle, and Rivington, 1881), 111–12; and Lewis Atherton, *Main Street on the Middle Border* (Bloomington: Indiana University Press, 1954), 223, cited in Young, *Toadstool Millionaires*.

20. Young, *Toadstool Millionaires*, 122.

21. Charles H. Pinkham, "Advertising 1875–1953," 172, The Lydia E. Pinkham Medicine Company Records, Schlesinger Library, Radcliffe Institute, Harvard University.

22. Young, *Toadstool Millionaires*, 209; and *Druggist Circular* 49 (1905): 30.

23. Young, *Toadstool Millionaires*, 195–96; Malcom Webber, *Medicine Show* (Caldwell, ID: Caxton Printers, 1941), 14, 47–48, 83–85; O. Henry, "Jeff Peters as a Personal Magnet," in *The Gentle Grafter* (New York: Doubleday, Page, 1908), 22; Charles L. Pancoast, *Trail Blazers of Advertising* (New York: Grafton Press, 1926), 178; and David Edstrom, "Medicine Man of the '80s," *Reader's Digest* 32 (June 1938): 77.

24. Brooks McNamara, *Step Right Up* (Garden City, NY: Doubleday, 1976), 16.

25. Ibid., 21–22.

26. Webber, *Medicine Show*, 24, 47–48.

27. Gregory J. Higby, "Chemistry and the 19th-Century American Pharmacist," *Bulletin for the History of Chemistry* 28, no. 1 (2003): 9–17, http://www.scs.illinois.edu/~mainzv/HIST/bulletin_open_access/v28-1/v28-1%20p9-17.pdf.

28. Elysa Ream Engelman, "'The Face That Haunts Me Ever': Consumers, Retailers, Critics, and the Branded Personality of Lydia E. Pinkham" (PhD diss., Boston University, 2003), 63; and "The Sin of Substitution," *The Pharmaceutical Era* 13, no. 14 (March 21, 1895): 417–18.

29. "The Department Store Octopus," *The Pharmaceutical Era* (May 23, 1895): 643; and "The Department Store," *The Pharmaceutical Era* (May 30, 1895): 673.

30. "Cutters Who Continue to Cut," *The Pharmaceutical Era* (January 30, 1896): 147; "These Cutters Discouraged," *The Pharmaceutical Era* (May 2, 1895): 562; "Cut-Prices in Syracuse," *The Pharmaceutical Era* (April 25, 1895): 531; and "Department Store Fight," *The Pharmaceutical Era* (April 4, 1895): 418, cited in Engelman, "Face That Haunts Me."

31. H. H. Roberts, as quoted in "Abuses of Proprietary Remedies," *The Pharmaceutical Era* (February 28, 1895): 259.

32. Conrad and Leiter, "From Lydia Pinkham," 827; and "Inflation Calculator," Dave Manuel.com, http://www.davemanuel.com/inflation-calculator.php.

33. Engelman, "Face That Haunts Me," 15.

5

The Vegetable Compound Takes Root

The Panic of 1873 sent shockwaves through American households, and in Lynn, few people were as shaken as Isaac Pinkham, who was never able to recover the money he had loaned. His fading health clouded his usually optimistic outlook, and as he approached 60, he quickly began to show his age. In his stead, Lydia and the other Pinkhams regrouped, addressing their financial situation and formulating plans that would turn an herb-based elixir she gave freely to neighbors into a high-demand product from which a dynamic company would spring.

First, they sold their house and moved to a small cottage on Western Avenue, where their Vegetable Compound factory would one day operate. Getting down to business, the brothers were fortunate they did not share their father's grandiose hopes or speculative nature.[1] Possessing a sound work ethic, they didn't shy away from making difficult choices. Their father's failed dreams notwithstanding, there was one lending move he made that helped the family lay claim to a formula whose ingredients were said to ease menstrual discomfort. Isaac had endorsed a note for Lynn machinist George Clarkson Todd, who defaulted and owed Isaac twenty-five dollars. In exchange for the payment, Todd gave him the formula, parts of which went into creating the mixture that became the Vegetable Compound.[2]

Just how much or how little of the formula was used is a matter of conjecture, with Lydia either adding its ingredients to her own and altering proportions or mixing them with ingredients found in her copy of John King's *The American Dispensatory*. King's work is a compilation of botanical information, with eighteen editions sold extensively in Europe and the United States.[3] Although grandson Charles in his company history "Advertising, 1875–1953" alludes that the compound was solely his grandmother's creation, Lydia's biographers assert that the compound formula was compiled from different sources, with at least some of Todd's ingredients being the only common thread.[4] Jean Burton, in *Lydia Pinkham Is Her Name*, went with the lore that said Lydia relied on King and on memories of ingredients brewed on the farm in her youth.[5] Dorry Baird Norris cited the King and Todd combination, while Robert Collyer Washburn favored the Todd–Lydia collaboration.[6]

A section from the 1870 edition of King's work (likely the edition Lydia may have used in her creation of the Vegetable Compound) referenced *Aletris farinosa* (unicorn root), which is listed as a tonic for the female generative organs.[7] The plant is indigenous to North America and is found south from Florida to Texas and as far north as Maine.[8] It is relatively small and has flowered stems, but the medicinal use is derived from the root.[9] Discussing the plant's merits, he noted, "In uterine diseases it may be given alone with advantage or employed in combination with [extracts]. It is of much utility in dyspepsia, as well as in cases of general or local debility." King also mentioned its benefits in regard to a prolapsed uterus and miscarriages, claims later often associated with the Vegetable Compound. In addition, King said the unicorn root could be combined with life root and pleurisy root, two other ingredients in Lydia's Vegetable Compound. He also stated the roots yield their curative properties best when steeped with alcohol.[10]

However it came together, here is the original formula for the Vegetable Compound according to Lydia's notebook:

Unicorn root (*Aletris farinosa* L.), 8 oz.
Life root (*Senecio aureus* L.), 6 oz.
Black cohosh (*Cimicifuga racemosa* L. Nutt.), 6 oz.
Pleurisy root (*Asclepias tuberosa* L.), 6 oz.
Fenugreek seed (*Trigonella foenum-graecum* L.), 12 oz.
Alcohol (18 percent), to make 100 pints[11]

One of the beauties of the compound was that it could have been made in almost any New England kitchen of the 1870s that had scales and cups. Most of the herbs Lydia used came finely ground from local suppliers, whom she relied on to harvest the plants when their natural juices were at their best. The herbs either were steeped, soaked in cold water, or macerated in diluted alcohol before the ingredients were mixed and put into a cloth bag. Prior to bottling the mixture, alcohol was added to act as a preservative, and the mixture was filtered through the cloth. Later, when distribution expanded, sifting machines extracted dirt, weeds, and grass, and wooden tanks to age the ingredients.[12]

The manufacturing process had to expand because the Pinkhams in 1875 decided there was money to be made from the concoction Lydia prepared in her kitchen and handed out to neighbors free of charge. "She used to just give it away to people who came to her," said descendant Caroline Doty. Family lore has it that the first sale was secured when a group of women traveled from Salem to Lynn to ask the Pinkhams if they could buy bottles of the Vegetable Compound. According to Doty, Lydia declined, but the women insisted she take five dollars for six bottles. "After that, my uncles said to her, 'Listen, if they have come from that far away to get that medicine, we might as well sell it.' And that's how it started."[13]

Emboldened by their initial transaction, the brothers established the price at the five-dollars-for-six-bottles mark, and word of mouth continued to bring people from miles away to make purchases. The Pinkhams put the first batch on the market in 1875 but did so knowing that they had to come up with ways to widen distribution because selling a patent medicine only in Lynn would not be easy. There were more than sixty manufacturers in Lynn alone, according to industry scholar Andrew Rapoza.[14] To no one's surprise, orders for the Vegetable Compound came in slowly at first, and the goal became to sell one bottle a day. Given the iffy nature of their new enterprise—the Lydia E. Pinkham Medicine Company—the brothers continued to work other jobs. The family designated Lydia as treasurer and general manager and decided to spend most of the early revenue on compound ingredients and initial advertising efforts.[15]

With the word *vegetable* in the name, the Pinkhams figured they had a sound product to market. From ancient times, the term carried a positive connotation. Hippocrates once prescribed, "Let food be your medicine and medicine be your food."[16] From her childhood, Lydia associated *vegetable* with *safe and reliable*, so connecting it with the compound seemed like a natural. At the time, other companies also promoted their cure-all drugs as being vegetable based, and the link has carried over to modern times.[17] Researchers, such as Mandip Sachdeva and Chandraiah Godugu of Florida A&M University as well as Stephen Safe of Texas A&M University, have found that various compounds derived from vegetables are effective in treating the most resistant type of breast cancer.[18] The mixtures also have been used to treat melanoma and gum disease.[19]

One thing that distinguished the Vegetable Compound in its day was its taste, which at best was an acquired one. Many customers remembered a dark and pungent liquid with a sharp, biting aftertaste, while others were slightly more generous. "If it was chilled, it tasted like Moxie," one said, alluding to an old-time, New England–based soda fountain drink.[20] Despite the potion's flavor shortcomings, consumers believed it was good for them, and orders began to pick up. Production, painstaking at first, eventually would become more efficient and economical.[21] As demand grew slowly, the nascent company and its owners would be stretched to their limits. In addition to cooking up the compound in a cellar kitchen reserved for that purpose, Lydia wrote the copy for handbills and labels. Nightly, the family gathered to bottle the medicine before it was packed for shipping in secondhand boxes supplied by a local grocer.

Among many tasks, the brothers distributed handbills house to house, initially in Lynn and then to outlying areas and to Boston, where on their best days each would hand out two thousand. Although few orders ensued, repeat purchases from neighbors and other customers held steady.[22] A sixteen-dollar order from a drugstore marked the first over-the-counter sale and was a key step in the compound's evolution.[23] By 1877, the family had earned enough money to expand handbill distribution (favored by Dan) and initiate newspaper advertising (advocated by Will), which would trigger immense growth and help make the product a household name.[24]

Early on, the enterprise primarily was a direct mail-order business until druggists began selling the compound on consignment. As checks trickled in, the brothers one by one gave up other jobs and devoted their lives to making the family's company a success.

Dan saw opportunities for promotions and sales in New York.[25] On May 3, 1876, he settled in a two-dollar-a-week room near Brooklyn's City Hall, bought a map, and began handing out 20,000 pamphlets in the neighborhood and in Manhattan. Promoting the remedy was not easy because many people, still suffering the effects of the Panic of 1873, were hesitant to buy anything except necessities. Dan decided he had to create demand by going door to door with his handbills and hired a twelve-year-old boy whom he paid sixty cents a day to help him. Dan justified the expense by explaining in a letter to the family that the child's

> mother is a dressmaker and knows a good many sick women and has commenced "to blow" for the medicine. If you can send me that keg full of medicine, I think it would be well for me to put it out in trial bottles here in Brooklyn and let her give it to parties she knows; we can't lose much, and I think it would be a grand good thing as it would get these Millinery Store-Keepers and dressmakers to guzzling it.[26]

Although the boy was reliable, Dan added an adult employee and shared his rationale in another letter:

> I hired a good man, today, to help me distribute, get agents, etc., one who knows a great many druggists, porters of hotels, horse-car conductors and others who can help about advertising. He went to work this morning and this afternoon he went over to see a porter of French's Hotel to get him to arrange things so we could advertise to advantage around there. I agreed to pay him $10 per week and think it will amount to something as he is a good fellow and has a large acquaintance.[27]

Dan and his two employees could hand out as many as 3,500 handbills on an average day, so many that he wrote to the family asking for more, mindful of the expense involved and quick to detail his strategy:

> When will you have the next 20,000 for Brooklyn as I want to shove them out before the other lot gets cold? I've been a little cautious about giving them out to men and women on the street, but I think I should if we got them low enough to be kind of free with them. I put out some pamphlets on Water St., N.Y. today, the worst St. in America. It's pretty hard telling how to put out in New York. . . . A Dutch druggist told me today this complaint was very prevalent among Dutch women. . . . Shall put some out this afternoon on the Bowery as I think that will pay us.[28]

Printing costs became one of the company's biggest expenses, so the brothers always looked for the best deal, at one point securing a price of eighty-five cents per one thousand pamphlets.[29] Always pushing ahead, Dan envisioned handbills in the millions: "If you can only keep me going, there's bound to be some trade pretty quick. Now you, Will and Charlie, better race with my getting the lowest bid for a million. We must throw ourselves this summer on pamphlets if we ever do. . . . You better rush another barrelful along. . . . KEEP ME SUPPLIED WITH PAMPHLETS."[30]

Although Brooklyn seemed a tough place to establish themselves, Dan suggested that every member of the Pinkham family could learn plenty from the city and apply that education to the business. In a letter home, he said,

> One reason I want some [others] out here is because you can learn so much in regard to the right amount of advertising . . . and I actually think if the whole family should move here [because] the learning and the sharpening of us all up during two years time would be worth thousands of dollars to us in this business which I think depends almost wholly on discernment, keenness and knowledge. Hang it! We've got to reduce this advertising down to a science and instead of so much brute force we've got to use our wits in getting up something original that will count greatly to our advantage. Hurry up and one of you come out here and we'll scheme something through that will lift us up *quickly*. When I again come to Lynn I want to dress as if I'd just bankrupted a *Rainbow*.[31]

Dan's hard work occasionally generated good news, but money always was an issue and a point of contention in his letters home. "I see by your letter that you are receiving orders from all around, so I suppose you feel pretty well in regard to the Med. Business," he said in one.[32] But in another his frustration boiled over when the family wouldn't spare him even two dollars:

> Just received your letter dated 20th and found no money in it. Now for God's sake how do you expect me to live in Brooklyn without sending me any more money? I've eaten my breakfast and it cost just 15 cents. While I'm working hard it takes 20 cents to make me a good square meal. I've got now in my pocket just twenty five cents left so today I shall eat 10 cents worth more and then have 15 cents left, not enough to work tomorrow.
>
> There is no use in writing, I actually can't spare 3 cents to buy a stamp with and cramp my guts. I have got to get a job at something else in order to keep my belly full. . . . For God's sake whose management is it that keeps me from having what I actually need. You ought certainly to have sent me $20.00 out of $24.00 you received from Jackson as I am prudent and won't spend it extravagantly.
>
> I should think you would know that my shoes are all out by this time. Now I will recite my expenses of yesterday to you.
>
> Breakfast 20¢
> Fare for myself and boy to N.Y. and back to Brooklyn 8¢
> Hoboken, New York and back 12¢
> Dinner for both 40¢
> Supper for me 15¢
> Wages paid him 60¢,
> $1.55.[33]

Every night, he would sew his shoes together and do his best to keep his only suit clean. Commenting about this, he said, "This business is tough on clothing. . . . I'm beginning to look so confounded seedy that I feel as though I ought to go into the country pasting up posters."[34] When it came to one of the Vegetable Compound's biggest customers, Grosvenor, Dan revealed, "Don't know yet whether Grosvenor has sold any or not. I don't like to go near him as I look so bad."[35]

Despite his poverty, Dan thrived in New York because of his urban nature. Social skills were among his best qualities. He could start a conversation with anyone and talked at ease with all kinds of people. To pass the time, he socialized with druggists, regardless of whether they carried the Vegetable Compound, which later proved to be a great advantage in selling it.[36] His experience in the retail trade and the political arena no doubt helped him to persuade potential customers. He was a quick study during his short time in Brooklyn and wanted to share face to face with the family what he'd learned. After lobbying Will and the others for his twelve-dollar fare home to Lynn, he embarked.[37]

During Dan's weeks away in New York, Will and Charles had carried on the business. At this point (1876), the firm was actually a proprietorship, operating under the name of William H. Pinkham. With money tight, Will was the only family member with a clear credit history.[38] Among the two brothers' many sacrifices, Charles walked the fourteen-mile roundtrip to save carfare when traveling to and from Salem.[39] He was still working for the railroad, which meant much of the Pinkham Company load fell to Will, who was considered the "mechanical minded" brother. He is credited with directing two key initiatives, one being the company's manufacturing process, which was considered very modern for the era.[40] The other was buying the first newspaper advertising for the remedy.

The company's original foray into advertising was an expensive proposition. Four-page circulars cost two dollars per thousand to print then had to be folded and distributed to 50,000 families, which cost an additional one hundred dollars. Although some of those costs came down, by the time another twenty-five dollars for carfare and lunches hit the bottom line, the balance sheet was out of kilter, and additional options had to be explored. One was the *Boston Herald*, which reached 50,000 homes more cheaply and would become just the vehicle the Pinkhams needed.[41]

The first *Herald* ads were sizable but did not include testimonials or Lydia's engaging portrait (they would come later). Rather, they featured text from the four-page circulars that promoted the compound as a cure-all for female complaints, as well as for kidney and bladder troubles. In need of money to pay for the ads, Will looked to Boston wholesale druggist Weeks and Potter, the Pinkhams' biggest customer, to collect eighty-four dollars for its most recent order. He used that to reproduce the circular on the front of the *Boston Herald* for sixty dollars. The rest of the family did not share Will's excitement because of doubts that so much money for a single ad in one newspaper would be worthwhile. Later, Lydia said, "That was like a thunderclap out of a clear sky, and we all sat down and had a good cry."[42] But when three different wholesalers ordered a gross of the Vegetable Compound, the thunderbolt paid off.

The newspapers' potential convinced the Pinkhams to offer their house as a form of security to the *Herald* for $1,000 worth of ads. They soon found that the increased business generated by this form of promotion covered what they owed.[43] With a newfound confidence, the Pinkhams looked to additional sources of security. Because real estate had not regained the value it held before the Panic of 1873, they used other properties as collateral. Dan noted, "So I guess real estate won't rise very quick. You had better work up everything in the shape of a mortgage into printing. Haven't you got any other mortgage you can turn? If we put many more mortgages into the business it does seem as if we ought to get easy money matters bye and bye."[44] A dramatic increase in compound orders helped the Pinkhams build their credit, making it easier to go into debt for materials and printing.[45] Newspaper advertising, mainly in Boston at first because of prohibitive costs in New York, became the company's main form of promotion but not the only one. Always looking to diversify, Dan also tried out a small advertisement in a religious publication because he thought the ad would "give a kind of religious tone to our Compound and get the good will of a few Methodists for it."[46]

Will pressed on and in 1878 met with the manager of the *Marblehead Messenger* (Massachusetts) newspaper. As the manager opened his morning mail, with disgust he threw one particular letter into the trash, a one-year contract promoting Hop Bitters from ad agent H. P. Hubbard through an agency in New Haven, Connecticut. Hubbard had proposed a rate so low that the executive feared his newspaper would be on the road to ruin had it accepted the offer. Impressed by Hubbard's strategy, Will decided that the agent would be the ideal man to promote the Vegetable Compound. At a meeting in Lynn, an advertising program was developed that featured a ten-inch layout in every paper in Connecticut and Rhode Island deemed worthy. The campaign would cost the Pinkhams $4,000 a year, an amount payable at a rate of $1,000 every three months.

Orders poured in, and the family paid for the entire year in just the first three months. Will instructed Hubbard to start advertising in Maine, and three months later, the campaign was extended to New Hampshire and Vermont. Massachusetts was next, and in ninety-day intervals that followed, the push began in eastern and western New York. Most of the advertising was confined to New England, but there is evidence that, as early as 1877, ads appeared in the *Indianapolis Sun*, the *Iowa State Register*, and the *Iowa State Leader*.[47] Word of the Vegetable Compound spread quickly.[48]

The message was getting out on other fronts, as well. Before Dan settled in Brooklyn, the versatile four-page circular had been expanded into a pamphlet, *A Guide for Women*, although Dan for a time removed the phrase from the cover, concerned that some folks might think it too "cheeky."[49] Printing costs were at $1.20 per 1,000, and Dan's goal was that, once the company's various promotions persuaded women to buy the potion, they would be able to find it at almost any drugstore. "We have no business to put out pamphlets anywhere in large cities, especially saying on them 'For Sale by all druggists' unless we put our medicine into all druggists," he told Will.[50]

By the fall of 1879, Dan had distributed more than one million pamphlets but was not content with his effort in the big cities, suggesting, "If I could only make Brooklyn and New York do as well in proportion as Concord, N.H., I should be satisfied."[51] In addition to distributing pamphlets, he used posters to promote the compound and had printers from New York to Chicago bidding on lots of 100,000.[52] Looking to reduce costs even further, he enlisted agents to advertise sales of washing and sewing machines, books, and clothes on the backs of pamphlets and got the agents to distribute the guides for free. An early cross-advertisement for a balsam, whose salesmen distributed the pamphlets in Brooklyn and upstate New York, saving both companies money.

Advertising cards, or trade cards, also were a popular medium of the day. Typically, a famous person, impressive scene, or pretty girl would adorn them. Dan had a different idea, proposing to include a message and then drop the ad pieces in resorts or parks late on a Saturday night so they could be read first thing Sunday morning. Dan once said, "Chelsea Beach would be a grand place to do this if the tide didn't come up over the resort, but there are plenty of places where it don't."[53] He also proposed to Will that cards be dropped in cemeteries prior to Decoration Day (now called Memorial Day): "Just try it . . . and I'll bet it will sell a few bottles."[54] Dan appreciated the cards' personal touch, telling Will, "I think they would surely attract attention; I never saw anything of the kind and if you fellows have a suggestion as good and cheap as this, just out with it."[55] This was Dan's most frequently used ad copy:

Lydia E. Pinkham's Vegetable Compound is a sure cure for all Uterine Difficulties and all other complaints incident to females. For Sale by P. Jackson, 511 Fulton St. From your cousin, Mary[56]

The cards also were distributed free at grocery store counters, with children often the biggest collectors. Later, cards were attached to the products so the collector would have to purchase the item, a tactic similar to one used by cigarette brands of the day.[57]

One problem with the trading cards was that paper pickers often would gather them up before anyone had a chance to read them. Dan's solution was to make the cards so small that paper pickers wouldn't bother with them. He revealed that "every card I get hold of I write something on, as if I was recommending the Compound to somebody and accidentally lost it."[58]

Dan's biggest success with trading cards would come later and involve the Brooklyn Bridge. For years, he had observed its construction and wondered if it would be possible to cover the bridge from end to end with an ad for the compound. His solution was to superimpose a message on a picture of the bridge and turn it into a card. During the next few years, more than a million Lydia Pinkham Brooklyn Bridge cards were distributed.[59] The trade piece, which debuted in the early 1880s, was one of the most noteworthy and successful Pinkham ads. When the trade card was removed from circulation in the 1890s, compound sales decreased 80 percent. When it returned a few years later, they increased almost 2,500 percent.[60] Coincidentally, Lydia died the same week in 1883 that the famous span opened.[61]

Amid all the promotional success, trouble brewed. As a relatively new trade, professional advertising oozed with bombast but lacked ethical standards. By 1878, newspaper publishers and editors had marked Hubbard as part blackmailer, part highwayman, and part conman. He was known for forcing advertising prices so low that it became difficult for newspapers to make a profit.[62] By 1881, Pinkham Company revenue wasn't covering advertising expenses. As the firm's advertising agent, Hubbard was purchasing large portions of newspaper space and reselling it to the Pinkhams at great personal profit. The family soon came to realize that the agent not only had become the company's largest creditor but had the power to take over the business. Presently, he would demand a share of ownership in exchange for the money owed him.

Will and Dan had performed remarkably in building the business to this point, but it came at a cost that took a great toll on their lives. Will led the newspaper advertising surge but was already showing signs of burnout in his late twenties. While in Brooklyn, Dan often went hungry and wore out his shoes. He spent his days handing out pamphlets, dropping cards in parks, and putting up posters. In short, he possessed a very strong drive to do whatever it took to make the Vegetable Compound successful, but he was all consumed.[63]

As Hubbard's power grew, Dan in one last blast proposed an idea that would reverse the company's fortunes. Believing that the Vegetable Compound's label was ineffective, he laid out a plan to the family in which a grandmotherly portrait of Lydia would become its central feature.[64] Her response was, "Do as you please, boys," which gave others the green light to create a brand that would become world famous and generate sales to millions.[65]

The portrait, which debuted on labels in the summer or fall of 1879, also appeared in a large lithograph form for distribution to druggists. The image adorned small cards on the reverse side of product ads, as well, and since then has been featured on almost everything the company has produced.[66] Prominent in drugstore windows, the portrait took on a life of its own. One newspaper noted, "Repeated requests have induced the proprietor of Lydia E. Pinkham's Vegetable Compound to send by mail to various lady correspondents large, mounted portraits of Mrs. Pinkham. Soon, many household walls were adorned by the familiar, motherly face of the Massachusetts woman who had done so much for all women."[67]

The image was reprinted with various degrees of clarity and detail, depending on the medium, with newspapers being the worst.[68] Legend has it that after an ad was placed in the *Boston Herald*, a makeup man got drunk and placed Lydia's picture at the top of every column in the paper.[69] Reportedly, there were even instances when editors, faced with needing a picture of a woman featured in a story, used Lydia's portrait as an alternative.[70]

Now on its way to achieving brand status, the Vegetable Compound became easier to promote. Dan exhorted Will, "I'm glad to see you are [covering it] so heavy down in Maine. I'd run that state to its full capacity so that anybody that sees any paper in the whole state will surely see our ad. [In Massachusetts] I'd advertise it so thoroughly that it could never die out."[71]

But even as sales and expectations escalated, the issues surrounding Hubbard would linger and mount. Within months, health concerns would sideline Dan and Will, pushing Charles to the company's forefront. Charles acted quickly in confronting Hubbard's ad markup scheme by halting all advertising. In March 1881, Charles also began negotiating with investor F. C. Cross of New Jersey, hoping that Cross would provide financial backing for the Pinkham Company and block the ad agent's power grab. Instead, Cross offered to buy the firm, which Charles used as a bargaining chip with Hubbard, who eventually yielded because he feared being out of a job if the Pinkhams sold.[72]

As that drama was playing out, another was unfolding. Dan and Will were out of commission, and all too soon they would be out of the picture.

One of the few men mentioned in Lydia's medical notebook was named Daniel, probably a reference to her son because she wrote that the individual was in New York at the time Dan was promoting the Vegetable Compound. Writing on December 19, 1878, Lydia recommended to an ill Daniel that he take three liver pills as well as a complex concoction of herbs and other ingredients. When Dan actually arrived home sick, Lydia advised another remedy, of pleurisy root and bugle weed, and that he be induced to sweat. He reportedly got better, but within a few years, his family again viewed him as a sick man without the same ambition and drive he once had.[73] Will, Charles, and others offered plenty of support, but that carried Dan only so long. At age thirty-two, he died in October 1881 at the Pinkham home on Western Avenue.

The entire Lynn community mourned him, and a local obituary noted, "He was considered one of the smartest scholars that ever graduated from the Lynn schools. In fact, he was one of the most brilliant men that Lynn ever sent forth."[74] For his six years of hard work promoting the Vegetable Compound and struggling with finances, he had only six months of financial security to show for it.[75] Although Lynn felt Dan's loss, his family felt it even more.[76]

The hardships did not end there for the Pinkhams. Within two months of Dan's death, Will became ill, and his health deteriorated. Emma, his young wife, took him to California to regain his strength, but the trip was not beneficial, and he died from quick consumption in December. Will was the closest to his mother, and his death at only twenty-eight was a huge blow. Her turn to spiritualism in later years may have been her way of coping.

The brothers' passing ushered in a new chapter for the company. Just after Dan died, the Pinkhams organized their business as a partnership for added security. The family always worried that Isaac's creditors would make claims, considering the compound's reach and its ability to generate revenue. When Dan died, Lydia and Isaac inherited his interest, which they quickly turned over to the surviving children.[77] Three shares were divided among Will, Charles, and Aroline. A short time later,

Will's share went to his wife, Emma Barry Pinkham, who died shortly thereafter in 1882, transferring it to her brother, Eugene Barry.[78] Strained relations between the remaining Pinkham children and Barry kept him out of the management picture.[79]

Even though Lydia distanced herself from company ownership, her face was so deeply associated with the brand that Isaac's creditors put pressure on her to pay his debts. She took a "Poor Debtor's Oath" in the spring of 1882, arriving at the court-house "riding in a magnificent coupe," according to the *Lynn Bee*. Other newspapers added embellishments that made it seem as though the business had failed. Despite the publicity, or perhaps because of it, the ensuing days of conversation in a way worked like an advertisement.[80]

In September 1882, the family transformed the company once again by incorporating it in Maine to take advantage of tax laws. Assets consisted mainly of equipment and supplies to create the compound but very little cash. Charles was elected general manager and president, with Aroline as treasurer and her husband as the secretary. The three comprised the board of directors. The company was valued at $11,200 and issued 112 shares of common stock. Charles and his sister each controlled forty-nine shares. Will Gove (now Aroline's husband) held one of her shares in a trust so he would qualify as an officer and director.[81] The other fourteen shares, a one-eighth interest in the company, went to Barry, who in a layered transaction sold the stock back to the family.[82]

With that resolved, Charles could return his attention to Hubbard and the question of whether the ad agent was committed to the company or to himself. In late 1883, Charles made a cross-country trip to meet with newspaper publishers to see if they had been paid on time and whether Hubbard had taken only the commissions the Pinkhams had granted him. Once Hubbard's dishonesty was revealed, Charles was in a quandary because he owed Hubbard too much money to fire him. But by halting advertising, Charles came up with a way to simultaneously meet the payments on the notes owed to Hubbard, while forcing the ad man to normalize his business practices. Signed on December 27, 1883, the settlement would "be considered as a healing of all differences which may have existed as to rates of commission . . . to the full satisfaction of both parties."[83] The focus could now be on promoting the compound.

Steadily over the years, advertising expenditures increased, rising to $200,000 annually by 1895. Lydia's fame was soaring, and revenue was starting to flow once again. But as so often seemed the case with the Pinkhams, contentment's visit to their household would last all too short a time. As her sons made their respective marks on the company, Lydia was busy making large batches of the compound while still doing housework and tending to Isaac's needs. A man broken by economic turmoil, Isaac mostly read aloud to himself, a shawl over his knees. The family, sensitive to his emotional and physical frailty, tried to make him feel needed by consulting him on big decisions. Lydia, in her sixties in the early 1880s, also made time to answer the people who wrote letters to her. But just as Isaac's condition improved and her load was about to lighten, Lydia suffered a paralytic stroke two days before

Christmas 1882. Confined to bed, she was attended to by a nurse, Aroline, and Marianna Estes, a relative. Over the next few months, for short periods of time, she seemed to be improving. Some days, she was moved out of her bedroom so she could sit up for an hour or two. But hopes of getting better soon gave way to faded spirits, and she said she "would rather be with them," referring to Dan and Will. One spring night Aroline remained beside her mother, who was patting her daughter's hand, saying, "My little girl, the only little girl I have got." A final "won't be here much longer" marked the end on May 17, 1883.[84]

In her last month, at age sixty-four, Lydia felt very close to Dan and Will, perhaps because of her strong sense of spiritualism. At her request, instead of prolonged mourning, her funeral was celebrated as a reunion with her sons. At the end of the service, old friend John Hutchinson, the last survivor of the "Singing Hutchinson Family," sang the refrain of "Almost Home."[85]

Perhaps because of the Lydia Pinkham Company's vast spending on advertising through the years, Lydia was very popular among newspaper men, in life and in death. Their respect was reflected in the obituaries and articles about her passing. The *New Haven Register* referred to her as the "model of matronly goodness and unbounded philanthropy." The paper advised those in the advertising community to cut out Lydia's picture and paste it to their hats as a tribute to the woman who did so much for advertising and for newspapers.[86] The *Macon Telegraph* advised newspaper men to mourn her death.[87] The *Duluth News Tribune* praised her achievements in advertising and called her a "rare woman."[88] The *Oregonian* declared, "Mrs. Pinkham was a liberal patron of the newspapers, and, of course, has gone straight to heaven."[89]

Some newspapers were not so cordial. The *Trenton Evening Times* remarked, "Now that Mrs. Lydia Pinkham is dead it is to be hoped that the numerous portraits of her that have been so extensively lavished upon newspapers will also be buried."[90] In another instance, *Times-Picayune* (New Orleans) claimed that a newspaper withheld eulogies for her while supposedly asserting, "Lydia Pinkham never brought blessings to this office. She always wanted too much room for the ducats."[91]

After Lydia's passing, Isaac went to live with the Goves in Salem. He again engaged in his real estate business, and the local paper wrote about him, saying he was "pleasantly passing the evening of his life in the midst of a prosperity which he can still aid by his counsel and advice." For six more years, Isaac enjoyed a gentle and quiet life, before his death in 1889. He was buried next to Lydia in Pine Grove Cemetery in Lynn, their union built on love and a belief in something bigger than themselves.[92]

NOTES

1. Jean Burton, *Lydia Pinkham Is Her Name* (New York: Little and Ives, 1949), 67–69; and Charles H. Pinkham, "Advertising 1875–1953," 1953, 4–5, The Lydia E. Pinkham Medicine Company Records, Schlesinger Library, Radcliffe Institute, Harvard University.

2. Sarah Stage, *Female Complaints: Lydia Pinkham and the Business of Women's Medicine* (New York: Norton, 1979), 27.

3. Burton, *Lydia Pinkham*, 51; and John King, *American Dispensatory*, 18th ed., (Cincinnati: Ohio Valley Co., 1898).

4. C. H. Pinkham, "Advertising 1875–1953," 5; Stage, *Female Complaints*, 27; and Robert Collyer Washburn, *The Life and Times of Lydia Pinkham* (New York: G. P. Putnam's Sons, 1931), 3–4.

5. Burton, *Lydia Pinkham*, 50–54.

6. Dorry Baird Norris, *Lydia Pinkham: Herbal Entrepreneur* (Franklin, TN: Sage Cottage, 1996), 5; and Washburn, *Life and Times*, 3–4.

7. Varro E. Tyler, "Was Lydia E. Pinkham's Vegetable Compound an Effective Remedy?" *Pharmacy in History* 37, no. 1 (1995): 24; and John King, *The American Dispensatory*, 8th ed. (Cincinnati: Wilstach, Baldwin, 1870), 78–79.

8. Tyler, "Vegetable Compound an Effective Remedy?" 24–28; and King, *American Dispensatory*, 8th ed., 78–79; and Frank D. Venning, *Wildflowers of North America: A Guide to Field Identification* (New York: St. Martin's, 2001), 40.

9. King, *American Dispensatory*, 8th ed., 78–79.

10. Tyler, "Vegetable Compound an Effective Remedy?" 24; King, *American Dispensatory*, 8th ed., 78–79.

11. Lydia E. Pinkham, "Medical Directions for Ailments," ca. 1878, vol. 538, 22, The Lydia E. Pinkham Medicine Company Records, Schlesinger Library, Radcliffe Institute, Harvard University; Burton, *Lydia Pinkham*, 107; and Harry Finley, "Patent Medicine Etc.: Lydia Pinkham," *Museum of Menstruation and Women's Health*, 2005, http://www.mum.org/mrspin17.htm.

12. "Process of Manufacture," 1, and "Making a Medicine," 2, 5, 7, both in MC 181, 2635, n.d., The Lydia E. Pinkham Medicine Company Records, Schlesinger Library, Radcliffe Institute, Harvard University.

13. Dan Yaeger, "The Lady Who Helped Ladies," *Yankee* 53, no. 9 (September 1989): 65–66.

14. Ibid., 65.

15. Burton, *Lydia Pinkham*, 70–72; and C. H. Pinkham, "Advertising 1875–1953," 6.

16. "Hippocrates Quotes," *Goodreads*, http://www.goodreads.com/author/quotes/248774. Hippocrates.

17. Henry G. Wright, "Vegetable Diet," lecture and discussion (January 24, 1843 to Freemans Institute, Lynn, MA), recorded in the minutes of the same association by Lydia Pinkham, secretary, "Notebook of Lydia E. Pinkham, including minutes of Freemans Institute, 1848–1865," folder 3365, frame 15 of seventy-seven scans in the author's possession, The Lydia E. Pinkham Medicine Company Records, Schlesinger Library, Radcliffe Institute, Harvard University; "Dr. Cooley's Vegetable Elixir," *Morning Chronicle* (New York), no. 723, February 8, 1805, 4; "Roger's Vegetable Pulmonic Detergent," *Portsmouth Oracle* (Portsmouth, NH), vol. 22, no. 30, April 27, 1811, 4; and "Vegetable Tooth Powder," *Georgian* (Savannah, GA), vol. 5, no. 66, February 12, 1824, 3.

18. "Vegetable Compounds Effective in Treating Triple-Negative Breast Cancer, Study Shows," *Huffington Post*, October 17, 2012, http://www.huffingtonpost.com/2012/10/17/vegetable-compounds-effective-triple-negative-breast-cancer_n_1975343.html.

19. "Fruit and Vegetable Compound Offers Hope against Gum Disease," *HealthCanal*, October 18, 2011, http://www.healthcanal.com/oral-dental-health/22004-Fruit-and

vegetable-compound-offers-hope-against-gum-disease.html; "Vegetable-Based Drug Could Inhibit Melanoma," *Phys.org*, March 1, 2009, http://phys.org/news155132202.html; and Ethan A. Huff, "Vegetable Compound May Prevent, Treat Arthritis," *Natural News*, September 16, 2010, http://www.naturalnews.com/029757_sulforaphane_arthritis.html.

20. Yaeger, "Lady Who Helped," 65.

21. "The Lydia E. Pinkham Plant, History of Mfg. Process," MC 181 2635, The Lydia E. Pinkham Medicine Company Records, Schlesinger Library, Radcliffe Institute, Harvard University.

22. Burton, *Lydia Pinkham*, 72–74; and Stage, *Female Complaints*, 33.

23. Cecil Munsey, "Lydia's Medicine, 130 Years Later," *CecilMunsey.com*, 2003, http://cecilmunsey.com/index.php?option=com_docman&task=doc_download&gid=788&&Itemid=34.

24. Burton, *Lydia Pinkham*, 80–81; and C. H. Pinkham, "Advertising 1875–1953," 9.

25. Burton, *Lydia Pinkham*, 74–75; and Washburn, *Life and Times*, 103.

26. Burton, *Lydia Pinkham*, 76–78; and C. H. Pinkham, "Advertising 1875–1953," 10.

27. Burton, *Lydia Pinkham*, 78–79.

28. Ibid., 79–80.

29. Ibid., 80.

30. Ibid., 81.

31. Washburn, *Life and Times*, 127–28.

32. Burton, *Lydia Pinkham*, 84.

33. Ibid., 97–98; and Stage, *Female Complaints*, 36.

34. Ibid., 101; and Stage, *Female Complaints*, 36.

35. Burton, *Lydia Pinkham*, 95.

36. Ibid., 93–94; and Stage, *Female Complaints*, 38.

37. Burton, *Lydia Pinkham*, 103.

38. C. H. Pinkham, "Advertising 1875–1953," 10, 22.

39. Washburn, *Life and Times*, 102.

40. C. H. Pinkham, "Advertising 1875–1953," 6, 8.

41. Ibid., 9.

42. Ibid.

43. Burton, *Lydia Pinkham*, 116; and Stage, *Female Complaints*, 37, 39.

44. Ibid., 117.

45. Burton, *Lydia Pinkham*, 117–18.

46. Washburn, *Life and Times*, 127.

47. C. H. Pinkham, "Advertising 1875–1953," 17–18, 31.

48. Ibid.

49. Ibid., 10.

50. Ibid., 13.

51. Ibid., 14.

52. Ibid.

53. Ibid.; and Typescripts: Daniel R. Pinkham, letters to Wm. Pinkham, 1876–1879, Box 181, Folder 3118, The Lydia E. Pinkham Medicine Company Records, Schlesinger Library, Radcliffe Institute, Harvard University.

54. Typescripts: Daniel R. Pinkham, letters to Wm. Pinkham, 1876–1879, Box 181, Folder 3118, The Lydia E. Pinkham Medicine Company Records, Schlesinger Library, Radcliffe Institute, Harvard University.

55. Ibid.

56. Ibid.

57. James B. Twitchell, *Twenty Ads That Shook the World: The Century's Most Groundbreaking Advertising and How It Changed Us All* (New York: Three Rivers, 2000), 30.

58. C. H. Pinkham, "Advertising 1875–1953," 15.

59. Ibid., 15–16.

60. Twitchell, *Twenty Ads*, 32.

61. "Lydia Pinkham; Brooklyn Bridge," *Trenton Evening Times*, published as the *Trenton Times* (Trenton, NJ), May 23, 1883, 2, col. 2.

62. Stage, *Female Complaints*, 95; and H. P. Hubbard, "The Story of Lydia Pinkham," *Fame* (November 1892): 2, typescript of magazine article found in MC 181, 3035, The Lydia E. Pinkham Medicine Company Records, Schlesinger Library, Radcliffe Institute, Harvard University.

63. C. H. Pinkham, "Advertising 1875–1953," 18, 20–22.

64. Burton, *Lydia Pinkham*, 102, 104–5; and Stage, *Female Complaints*, 40.

65. Ibid., 105.

66. C. H. Pinkham, "Advertising 1875–1953," 26; Stage, *Female Complaints*, 105; and Elysa Ream Engelman, "The Face That Haunts Me Ever: Consumers, Retailers, Critics, and the Branded Personality of Lydia E. Pinkham" (PhD diss., Boston University, 2003), 21–22.

67. Engelman, "Face That Haunts Me," 21–22.

68. Ibid., 23–24.

69. "Lynn's Lydia Pinkham: First Woman in Advertising," *The Daily Item* (Lynn, MA), August 27, 1993, 5, in vertical files of the Lynn (MA) Public Library, s.v., Biographies and Obituaries, Pinkham, Lydia.

70. Norris, *Lydia Pinkham*, 10.

71. C. H. Pinkham, "Advertising 1875–1953," 18.

72. Stage, *Female Complaints*, 96; and C. F. Cross to Charles H. Pinkham, March 4 and March 15, 1881, box 167, folder 3125, The Lydia E. Pinkham Medicine Company Records, Schlesinger Library, Radcliffe Institute, Harvard University.

73. Pinkham, "Medical Directions," 23.

74. Burton, *Lydia Pinkham*, 160.

75. Washburn, *Life and Times*, 166–67.

76. Burton, *Lydia Pinkham*, 160.

77. Stage, *Female Complaints*, 96, 99; "Partnership Agreement," October 18, 1881, box 164, folder 3043, The Lydia E. Pinkham Medicine Company Records, Schlesinger Library, Radcliffe Institute, Harvard University; and "Massachusetts, Deaths, 1841-1915," index and images, *FamilySearch* (https://familysearch.org/pal:/MM9.1.1/NW2H-KJK), Daniel R. Pinkham, (October 12, 1881); citing Lynn, Massachusetts, v 328 p 245, State Archives, Boston; FHL microfilm 960220; Daniel R. Pinkham death entry no. 628 (October 12, 1881), *Deaths Registered in the City of Lynn for the Year Eighteen Hundred and Eighty-one Lynn, Essex County, Massachusetts*, 1881, page 245, *Ancestry.com, Massachusetts, Death Records, 1841–1915* [online database] (Provo, UT: Ancestry.com Operations, 2013). Original data: *Massachusetts Vital Records, 1840–1911* (Boston: New England Historic Genealogical Society); and *Massachusetts Vital Records, 1911–1915* (Boston: New England Historic Genealogical Society), http://search.ancestry.com/search/db.aspx?dbid=2101.

78. Stage, *Female Complaints*, 99; William H. Gove to Charles H. Pinkham, October 17, 1884, box 168, folder 3133a; "Stock Certificates," box 164, folder 3047, The Lydia E.

Pinkham Medicine Company Records, Schlesinger Library, Radcliffe Institute, Harvard University; "Massachusetts, Deaths, 1841–1915," index and images, *FamilySearch* (https://familysearch.org/pal:/MM9.1.1/NW2H-LMJ), William H. Pinkham, (December 3 1881); citing Lynn, Massachusetts, v 328 p 248, State Archives, Boston; FHL microfilm 960220; William H. Pinkham, death entry no. 732 (December 3, 1881), in Los Angeles, California, as recorded in *Deaths Registered in the City of Lynn for the Year Eighteen Hundred and Eighty-one Lynn, Essex County, Massachusetts, 1881,* 248, *Ancestry.com, Massachusetts, Death Records, 1841–1915* [online database] (Provo, UT: Ancestry.com Operations, 2013). Original data: *Massachusetts Vital Records, 1840–1911* (Boston: New England Historic Genealogical Society); and *Massachusetts Vital Records, 1911–1915* (Boston: New England Historic Genealogical Society), http://search.ancestry.com/search/db.aspx?dbid=2101.

Emma F. Pinkham, death (April 29, 1882), Lynn, Essex County, Massachusetts, 1882 Ancestry.com. *Massachusetts, Death Records, 1841–1915* [database on-line]. Provo, UT, USA: Ancestry.com Operations, Inc., 2013. Original data: Massachusetts Vital Records, 1840–1911. New England Historic Genealogical Society, Boston, Massachusetts. Massachusetts Vital Records, 1911–1915. New England Historic Genealogical Society, Boston, Massachusetts. http://search.ancestry.com/search/db.aspx?dbid=2101.

79. C. H. Pinkham, "Advertising 1875–1953," 42.

80. Hubbard, "Story of Lydia Pinkham," 4.

81. Burton, *Lydia Pinkham*, 166–67; and C. II. Pinkham, "Advertising 1875–1953," 42–44.

82. C. H. Pinkham, "Advertising 1875–1953," 42–44.

83. Stage, *Female Complaints*, 98; and Agreement between Charles H. Pinkham and H. P. Hubbard, signed December 27, 1883, box 84, folder 763, The Lydia E. Pinkham Medicine Company Records, Schlesinger Library, Radcliffe Institute, Harvard University.

84. C. H. Pinkham, "Advertising 1875–1953," 18; and Burton, *Lydia Pinkham*, 206–7; and Lydia Pinkham (1819–1883), detail photograph of Pinkham memorial by Robert Rich, *Find A Grave Memorial*, no. 67034744 for Lydia Pinkham, http://www.findagrave.com/cgi-bin/fg.cgi?page=pv&GRid=818&PIpi=80141, accessed November 24, 2014.

85. John Wallace Hutchinson, *Story of the Hutchinsons: Tribe of Jesse* (Boston: Lee and Shepard, 1896), 2:110.

86. "Lydia Pinkham; Paralysis," *New Haven Register*, published as the *New Haven Evening Register* (New Haven, CT), vol. 61, no. 119, May 19, 1883, 2.

87. "Lydia Pinkham," *Macon Telegraph*, published as the *Telegraph and Messenger* (Macon, GA), no. 10373, May 20, 1883, 2, col. 1.

88. "Lydia Pinkham Is Dead," *Duluth News Tribune*, published as the *Duluth Daily Tribune* (Duluth, MN), vol. 3, no. 7, May 22, 1883, 2.

89. "Our Sisters, Our Cousins, and Our Aunts," *Oregonian*, published as the *Sunday Oregonian* (Portland, OR), June 29, 1883, 6.

90. "Mrs. Lydia Pinkham," *Trenton Evening Times*, published as the *Trenton Times* (Trenton, NJ), May 21, 1883, 2, col. 2.

91. "Lydia Pinkham," *Times-Picayune*, published as the *Daily Picayune* (New Orleans, LA), June 24, 1883, 4.

92. Burton, *Lydia Pinkham*, 207–8; and Isaac Pinkham (1815–1889), detail photograph of Pinkham memorial by Alex (no. 47424643), *Find A Grave Memorial*, no. 67034744 for Isaac Pinkham, http://www.findagrave.com/cgi-bin/fg.cgi?page=gr&GRid=67034744, accessed September 8, 2014.

6

Portrait of a Woman Who Led the Way

Lydia Pinkham was not only the face of her company, she was its heart and soul. When the compound was first marketed, she was fifty-six, making her much older than most women (or men) of the day who embarked on a new venture. Her place at the forefront also was emblematic of how women were taking even larger steps in the business world, creating and developing products, then taking those goods to market.[1]

By circumstance, she had to do it all. In the product's early days, Lydia not only composed ads and produced the remedy in a kitchen but also recorded sales information in her medical notebook and detailed the advice she offered her clientele. Although as early as 1878 she was sending the compound in pill form to numerous women, men were among her customers, too, including Arthur Lane, who had kidney trouble.[2]

With the compound's growing popularity, many women wrote to Lydia. As more did, she simply did not have the time to answer every letter, so she hired "lady type-writers" to address the letters the same way she would. Some of these testimonial letters would later serve as highly effective ads.[3] As if all that weren't enough, her image became a world-famous brand that personified the company and its product for years to come.

Just why that came about is yet another part of the Pinkham lore. That's because there are actually three versions of how her portrait launched the family's fortunes. One story begins with Dan noticing his mother's appearance upon returning from his travels. The idea struck him that the public might be attracted to a grandmotherly image, even though no company previously had used an older woman's photograph in an advertisement. He related the idea to Charles and Will, who agreed with his reasoning.[4]

Advertising agent Hubbard offered his own version, in which he credited himself with the idea:

> Mrs. Pinkham personally was a lady of very comely appearance, with a benign and motherly cast of countenance; her expression revealed natural refinement and general intelligence, and in a happy moment I conceived the idea that her motherly looking face put at the head of the advertisement would make it remarkably attractive. After some persuasion I obtained permission to use it.[5]

In his history of the Vegetable Compound and the Pinkhams, Hubbard expanded on the significance of his contribution:

> Did anybody notice it in the papers? Charles Goodwin, of C. C. Goodwin & Co., said that it tripled the value of the trademark at once, as it boomed the sales immensely, and about six months later they were offered $100,000 for the business and trademark. [Shoe manufacturer William Lewis] Douglas and others began to show their faces in the papers. In some cases Mrs. Pinkham and Douglas would appear in adjoining columns![6]

A third version has it that a newspaper article in 1881 headlined "Plucky Pinkhams" explained that widespread mistrust of patent medicines' promises made creating effective advertisements extremely difficult, so those who saw a Lydia Pinkham advertisement may have doubted she even existed. Because a photograph of her had just been taken, the brothers reasoned that, if her portrait were engraved and printed in the advertisements, the image would ease people's fears.[7]

Curiously, the portrait became a success because it played on a great many stereotypes that alleviated people's concerns about the Vegetable Compound. Although stereotypes have often held back women in business, Lydia's image personified a trustworthy figure and worked to the company's advantage.[8]

Other patent medicine advertisers used images of scantily clad American Indian maidens, fire-breathing dragons, or intrepid explorers to grab attention. Lydia's picture represented a commonplace, everyday person to which consumers could relate more easily. Images of other individuals during this time period placed a greater emphasis on attractive features, while Lydia's image was considered more akin to a "real woman."

Lydia was not the first person to have his or her name and likeness associated with a product. In fact, it was quite commonplace in her day. Other portraits also helped sell items, but Lydia's differed chiefly because of her sex. Starting in 1879, engravings were included in Pinkham Company advertisements, which probably is one of the main factors that led to an increase in sales.[9]

During its long lifespan, her portrait would experience cosmetic changes at the hands of several generations of Pinkham advertising managers. They would try to update the familiar figure by altering her clothing and hair or smoothing out a few wrinkles. But whether the image appeared in an 1880s advertisement or on a 1950s stationery letterhead, it retained the original *carte de visite* quality and remained a convincing likeness of the real Lydia Estes Pinkham.[10]

On other levels, she inspired women to confront what passed as reality. Many of the Vegetable Compound advertisements challenged the image many had of ladies during the Victorian Era. Lydia expounded, "Volumes are written these days about the duties of women, but the real gospel of women's success is the gospel of health." Commenting about menopause, she explained, "There is no period in woman's career which she approaches with so much anxiety as the 'change of life.'" Lydia regarded the anxiety as unnecessary, explaining,

> It is surprising what happy changes Lydia E. Pinkham's Vegetable Compound brings about in this condition. So marked is its power that all the trying days of the Change may be passed over in perfect safety. Women who have been dreading the Change, who have been taught to look upon it as something horrible, may now lay all such anxiety aside. Thousands of letters from women tell me that their life of distress and sleeplessness was changed to one of perfect comfort almost immediately.[11]

Lydia recommended that, in addition to taking the compound, women also should adopt healthy habits to alleviate their ailments. In one example, she said, "Bathe yourself all over every night in hot water. . . . Eat farinaceous food and broths. . . . Ride out and walk out; dig, use the trowel. When in the house sit by [an] open window (well protected) that you may inhale all the outdoor air possible." To these same women, she wrote this in reference to the compound: "I would not have you take my liquid for although there is only a sufficient quantity of alcohol in it to keep it that little would be bad for you. My Compound in dry form is good for you; its cleansing and healing properties will benefit you."[12]

There were cases, though, when Lydia felt that her remedy would not be enough. For instance, in her medical notebook, she wrote directions to alleviate the pain when the "stomach and liver is in so bad a condition that the Comp. will not benefit," recommending gentian root and additional unicorn root. It is also interesting to note that, despite her temperate views on alcohol, she prescribed "one gill of whiskey" to be added to fight the stomach and liver problems.[13]

In another revealing entry recorded in her medical notebook, Lydia noted that a Brooklyn woman named Mrs. Simpson took the Vegetable Compound and did not experience any benefit: "Comp. caused great distress in [Mrs. Simpson's] back. The Compound helping the uterus threw the humors upon the kidneys which is an unusual occurrence it generally relieving the back ache." This perplexed her, and based on her notes, it appears she couldn't find an explanation.[14]

Some of Lydia's advice to individuals might seem quite strange today. A woman's husband wrote to her complaining that his wife (name not listed) suffered from ovarian troubles and had been sick for three years. One of Mrs. Pinkham's recommendations included abstaining from drinking milk and instead consuming tea.[15]

Although individuals seeking medical advice often were ambiguous about their symptoms, Lydia tried to make specific suggestions. In one instance, she wrote about a woman by the name of J. C. Chandler of Medford, Massachusetts, who a doctor said had an enlargement of the womb. Lydia came to the conclusion that the correspondent had an ovarian sac filled with water.[16] In any event, she was consistent in recommending that women not submit themselves to surgery.[17]

In another revealing notebook entry, Lydia claims that "1 part carbolic acid 2 parts rose water for a wash will cure a cancer."[18] She also had simple directions for curing a headache, recommending a tablespoonful of lemon juice a half hour before every meal.[19] A remedy for small pox called for simply consuming cream of tartar. Regarding this cure, she asserted, "I have this from good authority."[20] Also in the notebook was an unidentified clipping that addressed how to approach certain medical situations. This indicates she was willing to seek outside information about women's health issues.[21] Scratched-out sentences and words in her notebook also showed she was open to tinkering with and revising her concoctions.[22]

As for the notion that women were meant to suffer, Lydia had this to say:

> Tradition says, "Women must suffer," and young girls taught so. There is a little truth and a great deal of exaggeration in this. The mother suffered and she thinks her daughter must suffer also. It is true only to a limited extent. No excessive pain is healthy. If a young woman suffers severely she needs treatment, and her mother should see that she gets it.[23]

Her personal life, however, was not free of suffering, with three of her sons preceding her in death and husband Isaac falling ill in his later years. Perhaps as a survival mechanism, her embrace of spiritualism led her to say in the notebook, "The spiritualists do not threaten with anything. They say 'Investigate and judge for yourselves.' The spiritualists are friends of political and social liberty." She also included a list of important men and women who believed in spiritualism, seemingly as a way to add support to her beliefs. Lydia and Isaac liked to sit side by side near the fire and wait for messages from the beyond or otherwise engage themselves in their two remaining children's lives.[24]

Amid the sorrow, royalties from the compound meant that by 1882 Lydia and Isaac were living comfortably. Even though she had become well known and enjoyed a celebrity-like status, Lydia managed to live frugally, remain modest, and be in good spirits.[25]

Even in her later years, Lydia showed ambition while continuing to work hard. Concerned that her advertisements were not conveying everything she wanted women to know, she decided to write her now-famous *Guide to Health*, which finally became *Lydia E. Pinkham's Private Textbook upon Ailments Peculiar to Women*. Lydia worried that many females were ignorant of their anatomies and general health. The fact they had few outlets to consult about their bodies distressed her. She wanted to contribute to the general health and welfare of society, asserting, "The women of this country must have physical education, if we are to have a people strong and hearty."[26] Although the book promoted the compound, its main purpose was to inform. The company handed out the book for free—the only work of its kind offered to the public without cost. Only later would the government issue similar information on child training, prenatal and postpartum care, and other subjects regarding women's health. The book became so popular that it was reissued under a number of different titles for years after her death.[27] By 1920, 11 million copies of the work were published each year. Lydia's great-grandson Charles later remarked, "It must have rivaled the Bible, with the number . . . printed over the years."[28]

Although the book was helpful in many ways, today its advice would not necessarily be prescribed by doctors. The volume contained many scientific terms and other information that would not typically be known to anyone outside the medical community of her day.[29]

In late December, just months before her death, Lydia reacquainted with old friend Frederick Douglass when he came back to Lynn to lecture. She was no longer the young woman who once had accompanied him on the train so many years ago; nonetheless her progressive views remained as strong as ever.[30] Although the Pinkhams and the world lost a remarkable woman with her passing, she lived on for generations, through her product, her writing, and a life lived in full.

NOTES

1. John McDonough and Karen Egolf, eds., "Pharmaceuticals," *The Advertising Age Encyclopedia of Advertising*, vol. 3, *P–Z* (New York: Fitzroy Dearborn, 2003), 1221.

2. Lydia E. Pinkham, "Medical Directions for Ailments," ca. 1878, vol. 537, 5, 18, The Lydia E. Pinkham Medicine Company Records, Schlesinger Library, Radcliffe Institute, Harvard University.

3. Jean Burton, *Lydia Pinkham Is Her Name* (New York: Little and Ives, 1949), 139–40; and Lydia E. Pinkham, *Lydia E. Pinkham's Private Text-Book upon Ailments Peculiar to Women.* Lynn, (MA: Lydia Pinkham Medicine Co., 1905), 110–111.

4. Ibid., 104–5; and Charles H. Pinkham, "Advertising 1875–1953," 1953, 24, The Lydia E. Pinkham Medicine Company Records, Schlesinger Library, Radcliffe Institute, Harvard University.

5. C. H. Pinkham, "Advertising 1875–1953," 26.

6. H. P. Hubbard, "The Story of Lydia Pinkham," *Fame* (November 1892): 3, typescript of magazine article found in MC 181, 3035, The Lydia E. Pinkham Medicine Company Records, Schlesinger Library, Radcliffe Institute, Harvard University.

7. C. H. Pinkham, "Advertising 1875–1953," 26.

8. Angel Kwolek-Folland, *Incorporating Women: A History of Women and Business in the United States* (New York: Twayne, 1998), 196.

9. Elysa Ream Engelman, "The Face That Haunts Me Ever: Consumers, Retailers, Critics, and the Branded Personality of Lydia E. Pinkham" (PhD diss., Boston University, 2003), 19–20; and Hubbard, "Story of Lydia Pinkham," 3.

10. Engelman, "Face That Haunts Me," 20–22.

11. Burton, *Lydia Pinkham*, 182–83; and *Lydia E. Pinkham's Private Text-Book*, 10

12. Pinkham, "Medical Directions," 59–60.

13. Ibid., 20.

14. Ibid., 24.

15. Ibid., 25–26.

16. Ibid., 28.

17. Ibid., 62.

18. Ibid., 35.

19. Ibid., 40.

20. Ibid., 69.

21. Ibid., 84–85.

22. Ibid., 22.

23. "The Duty of Mothers," *The Sacred Heart Review*, Vol. 19, 23, June 4, 1898.

24. Burton, *Lydia Pinkham*, 163–64, 205–6; and Sarah Stage, *Female Complaints: Lydia Pinkham and the Business of Women's Medicine* (New York: Norton, 1979), 26, 43

25. Ibid., 198.

26. Ibid., 184–85; and Dan Yaeger, "The Lady Who Helped Ladies," *Yankee* 53, no. 9 (September 1989): 67.

27. Ibid.

28. Yaeger, "Lady Who Helped," 67.

29. Burton, *Lydia Pinkham*, 185.

30. Burton, *Lydia Pinkham*, 204–5; and Frederick Douglass, *Life and Times of Frederick Douglass* (Boston: De Wolfe, Fiske, 1895), 279.

Lydia's hometown view in Lynn, Mass., 1856, the birthplace of the Vegetable Compound. Bachelder, J.B. "Lynn Massachusetts detailed birds-eye view," 1856, "Endicott & Co., lithographers (New York, 19th Century) Lot of Four "Album of New England Scenery" Views: Swampscott, Mass." Viewable at http://www.skinnerinc.com/auctions/2494/lots/615.

A Vegetable Compound ad that demonstrated the new working woman of the late 19th century and the hardships she faced as a result of female ailments and suffering on the job. In addition, this advertisement details the lack of understanding on the part of males as seen by the woman's frustrated boss. "Lydia E. Pinkham's Vegetable Compound," *The Daily Inter Ocean*, Chicago, IL, (February 18, 1891), Issue 330, 3, col. F.

A 19th-century doctor performing an examination on his female patient. His eyes are diverted so as to uphold the morals and modesty of the day. Maygrier, J. Pierre, *Nuove Dinostrazioui di Ostetricia*, (1831), reprinted *Midwifer Illustrated*, NY: Moore & Page, 1833, 29. Translated from the French, with notes by A. Sidney Doane, MD; "The Touch: Medicine in the 19th century," Victoriana, http://www.victoriana.com/doors/doctor.html

Lydia creating and bottling the Vegetable Compound in the early days of selling the concoction. Robert Collyer Washburn, *The Life and Times of Lydia E. Pinkham*, 1931, (G. P. Putnam's Sons: New York and London) Image between pages 12 and 13.

Trade card from 1883 that features the Brooklyn Bridge adorned with a Lydia Pinkham banner advertisement. However, the banner was never actually made or hung on the bridge. The image below is of the reverse side of the trade card, in which the usual price and benefits of using the compound are featured. Harry Finley, "Lydia Pinkham," *Patent Medicine, Etc.,* 2005, http://www.mum.org/MrsPink2.htm; and C. H. Pinkham, "Advertising 1875–1953," 16.

LYDIA E. PINKHAM'S
VEGETABLE COMPOUND
IS A POSITIVE CURE
For all those painful Complaints and Weaknesses so common to our best female population.

It will cure entirely the worst form of Female Complaints, all Ovarian troubles, Inflammation and Ulceration, Falling and Displacements, and the consequent Spinal Weakness, and is particularly adapted to the Change of Life.

It will dissolve and expel tumors from the uterus in an early stage of development. The tendency to cancerous humors there is checked very speedily by its use.

It removes faintness, flatulency, destroys all craving for stimulants, and relieves weakness of the stomach. It cures Bloating, Headaches, Nervous Prostration, General Debility, Sleeplessness, Depression and Indigestion.

That feeling of bearing down, causing pain, weight and backache, is always permanently cured by its use.

It will at all times and under all circumstances act in harmony with the laws that govern the female system.

For the cure of Kidney Complaints of either sex this Compound is unsurpassed.

LYDIA E. PINKHAM'S VEGETABLE COMPOUND is prepared at 233 and 235 Western Avenue, Lynn, Mass. Price $1. Six bottles for $5. Sent by mail in the form of pills, also in the form of lozenges, on receipt of price, $1 per box for either. Mrs. Pinkham freely answers all letters of inquiry. Send for pamphlet. Address as above.

No family should be without *LYDIA E. PINKHAM'S LIVER PILLS.* They cure constipation, billiousness, and torpidity of the liver. 25c. per box. — FOR SALE BY

HENRY D. CUSHMAN,
Three Rivers, Mich.

One of the responses Lydia wrote to an individual recommending the Vegetable Compound and Liver Pills for her complaints. *Advertisements in Periodicals,* Vol. VIII, 1924–1929 [advertisements actually go up to 1930], Lydia E. Pinkham Medicine Company, The Lydia E. Pinkham Medicine Company Records, Schlesinger Library, Radcliffe Institute, Harvard University.

The famous Lydia Pinkham portrait that graced countless numbers of ads taken from a 1914 pamphlet. "Women's Letters," Pinkham pamphlets, MC 181, 2431, Mail distribution, 1914, no. 83, back cover, The Lydia E. Pinkham Medicine Company Records, Schlesinger Library, Radcliffe Institute, Harvard University.

The actual painted portrait of Lydia Pinkham that became the basis of so many of the Vegetable Compound promotional pieces. B. Gordon, *Lydia E. Pinkham,* original painting in Schlesinger Library, Radcliffe Institute, Harvard University.

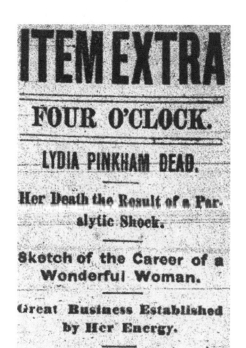

ITEM EXTRA

FOUR O'CLOCK.

LYDIA PINKHAM DEAD.

Her Death the Result of a Paralytic Shock.

Sketch of the Career of a Wonderful Woman.

Great Business Established by Her Energy.

One of the many obituaries for Lydia Pinkham. Most newspapers praised Lydia and her life's work since the Vegetable Compound contributed to these papers a great deal of income as a result of the large volume of advertising. "Lydia Pinkham Dead," *Daily Evening Item* (Lynn, MA) (May 18, 1883), 1.

The gravesite of Lydia Pinkham, with her husband Isaac. Dan and Will appear behind the monument at Pine Grove Cemetery in Lynn, MA. Bette Keva, Pine Grove Cemetery, Hackmatack Avenue, Lot 1343, Grave 8, Lydia, Lynn, MA, 2012.

The Lydia E. Pinkham Laboratory on Western Ave. in Lynn, MA. The building on the right still stands today as it was. "Help for Women," Pinkham Pamphlets, MC 181, 2427, 1910, no. 66, back cover, The Lydia E. Pinkham Medicine Company Records, Schlesinger Library, Radcliffe Institute, Harvard University.

One of the advertisements involving Lydia portrayed as a living person. At the time of this ad Lydia had been dead for more than seven years, but still managed to hold a conversation with one of her sons. "No Title," The Boston Herald (June 6, 1890), 1; Advertisements in Periodicals, Vol. I, 1890–1900, Lydia E. Pinkham Medicine Company, The Lydia E. Pinkham Medicine Company Records, Schlesinger Library, Radcliffe Institute, Harvard University.

This portion of an ad depicts a woman who became too ill to work. To help alleviate illness, the Vegetable Compound was promoted as a helpful agent. "I am not well enough to work," *The Boston Herald* (July 8, 1890) 1; *Advertisements in Periodicals,* Vol. I, 1890–1900, Lydia E. Pinkham Medicine Company, The Lydia E. Pinkham Medicine Company Records, Schlesinger Library, Radcliffe Institute, Harvard University.

The Writing Room at the Lydia Pinkham Company, hosted numbers of women who recommended steps to help females seeking advice. William H. Helfand, "Historical Images of the Drug Market-XXXVII," *Pharmacy in History. American Institute of the History of Pharmacy,* (1991), vol. 35, no. 1, 42–43.

WISE ADVICE TO HUSBANDS.

Those Who Have Ailing Wives Will do Well to Accept It.

Do not wrangle and quarrel, and finally rush into the courts and try to get a separation from your faithful wife; but just stop a moment and think! Your wife, who was even-tempered and amiable, and all that was lovely when you married her, has changed. Now she is peevish, irritable, jealous, discontented and miserable—in a word, she has uterine disorder of some kind.

Law is not the remedy for this condition, she needs medical treatment, her uterine system is at fault.

My advice to you is, sit down and write a letter to that friend of women, Mrs. Pinkham, of Lynn, Mass., state fully and freely the whole case to her and she will honestly advise you what to do. Give your wife that chance, good man!

If you do not wish to write about your wife, bring her a bottle of Lydia E. Pinkham's Vegetable Compound, watch its effects, you will soon see the beginning of the improvement; then get her another and keep it up until she is restored to you, the same lovely woman you married years ago.

Following we relate the circumstances of a case of this nature. Mrs. MELVA ROUTON, of Camby, Ind., says:

"I have used Lydia E. Pinkham's Vegetable Compound and found it to be of great benefit to me. The doctors said I had womb trouble. I had the headache all the time, also a terrible backache, was nervous, cross and irritable. I looked so pale that people would ask me what was the matter. I suffered in this way for about four years, until one day about in despair my husband brought me a bottle of Lydia E. Pinkham's Vegetable Compound. I commenced its use, and much to every one's surprise, it cured me. It has completely changed my disposition for the better also. Several of my neighbors, knowing what the Pinkham medicine has done for me, are taking it, and are much pleased with the result."

One of the Lydia Pinkham ads aimed at husbands, asking them to help understand their wife's ailments. "Wise Advice to Husbands," *Ohio Farmer* (April 1, 1897), 273.

MRS. PINKHAM TALKS ABOUT OVARITIS.

Letter from Mrs. Carrie F. Tremper that all Suffering Women Should Read.

An advertisement that dealt with specific ailments. This ad warns women of the dangers surrounding ovaritis, recommending the Vegetable Compound to fight the ailment. "Mrs. Pinkham talks about Ovaritis," *Massachusetts Ploughman and New England Journal of Agriculture*, (October 22, 1898), 58, 4, 6.

Ovaritis or inflammation of the ovaries may result from sudden stopping of the monthly flow, from inflammation of the womb, and many other causes. The slightest indication of trouble with the ovaries should claim your instant attention. It will not cure itself, and a hospital operation with all its terrors may easily result from neglect.

The fullest counsel on this subject can be secured without cost by writing to Mrs. Pinkham, at Lynn, Mass., and asking for her advice. Your letter will be confidential and seen by women only.

Mrs. CARRIE F. TREMPER, Lake, Ind., whose letter we print, is only one of many that have been cured of ovarian troubles by Lydia E. Pinkham's Vegetable Compound.

"DEAR MRS. PINKHAM:—I was suffering from congestion of the ovaries, misplacement of the womb, irregular, scanty, and painful menstruation, also kidney trouble. I had let it go on until I could not sit up, and could not straighten my left leg. My physician gave me relief, but failed to cure me. Reading the testimonials of different women, telling what Lydia E. Pinkham's Vegetable Compound had done for them, I decided to give it a trial. I had almost given up hopes, as I had suffered untold agony. The first dose helped me. And now, after using eight bottles of Vegetable Compound, one bottle of Blood Purifier, one box of Liver Pills, I am proud to say I am as well as I ever was. I might have saved a large doctor's bill and much suffering, had I tried your precious medicine in the beginning of my sickness. All in the village know I was not expected to live, when I had the first and second attacks. In fact, I had no hope until I began taking your Vegetable Compound. It has saved my life."

A Million Women Have Been Benefited by Mrs. Pinkham's Advice and Medicine

This part of a Pinkham ad addressed the subject of sterility and how the compound can lead to the birth of a child. "If we only had Children!," *Boston Herald*, published as *The Sunday Herald*, (May 25, 1890), 28; *Advertisements in Periodicals*, Vol. I, 1890–1900, Lydia E. Pinkham Medicine Company, The Lydia E. Pinkham Medicine Company Records, Schlesinger Library, Radcliffe Institute, Harvard University.

"I am a Living Witness of the Wonderful and Miraculous Effects of Lydia E. Pinkham's Vegetable Compound."

Part of an advertisement that encouraged women to write to Lydia to share their testimonials. "I am a Living Witness of the Wonderful and Miraculous Effects of Lydia E. Pinkham's Vegetable Compound," *The North American* (Philadelphia, PA) (April 2, 1896), 6.

On the right is another example of a Pinkham trade card from the late 1880s. Below is the reverse of that card, which makes the reader aware of the Vegetable Compound as well as the Blood Purifier. Belle Waring, "Commodification Meets Black Cohosh," NLM Seminar Focuses on 19th-Century Patent Medicine, (April 7, 2006), http://nihrecord.od.nih.gov/newsletters/2006/04_07_2006/story04.htm; "Chromolithograph," Boston Public Library, Print Department, http://en.wikipedia.org/wiki/File:Lydia_E._Pinkhams_cures_and_claims.jpg

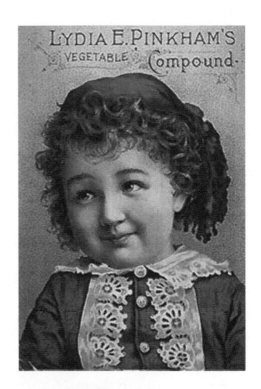

LYDIA E. PINKHAM'S
VEGETABLE COMPOUND
IS A POSITIVE CURE

For all those painful Complaints and Weaknesses so common to our best female population.

It will cure entirely the worst forms of Female Complaints, all Ovarian troubles, Inflammation, Ulceration, Falling and Displacements of the Womb, and the consequent Spinal Weakness, and is particularly adapted to the Change of Life.

It will dissolve and expel Tumors from the Uterus in an early stage of development. The tendency to cancerous humors there is checked very speedily by its use. It removes faintness, flatulency, destroys all craving for stimulants, and relieves weakness of the stomach. It cures Bloating, Headaches, Nervous Prostration, General Debility, Sleeplessness, Depression and Indigestion.

That feeling of bearing down, causing pain, weight and backache, is always permanently cured by its use.

It will at all times and under all circumstances act in harmony with the laws that govern the female system. For the cure of Kidney Complaints of either sex this Compound is unsurpassed.

Lydia E. Pinkham's Vegetable Compound is prepared at Lynn, Mass. Price, $1.00; six bottles for $5.00. Sent by mail in the form of Pills, also in the form of Lozenges, on receipt of price, $1.00 per box, for either. Send for pamphlet. All letters of inquiry promptly answered. Address as above.

No family should be without LYDIA E. PINKHAM'S LIVER PILLS. They cure Constipation, Biliousness, and Torpidity of the Liver. 25 cents per box.

Lydia E. Pinkham's Blood Purifier.

This preparation will eradicate every vestige of Humors from the Blood, and at the same time will give tone and strength to the system.

It is far superior to any other known remedy for the cure of all diseases arising from impurities of the blood, such as Scrofula, Rheumatism, Cancerous Humors, Erysipelas, Canker, Salt Rheum and Skin Diseases.

SOLD BY ALL DRUGGISTS.

Compliments of

This Vegetable Compound ad (1901–1902) is focused on the subject of motherhood but note the insert in the top right corner, which promised a $5,000 reward if any of the testimonials were found to be false. The purpose of this became to combat the growing number of skeptics and muckrakers of the time. "Joyful Maternity," *Advertisements in Periodicals*, Vol. II, 1901–1902, Lydia E. Pinkham Medicine Company, The Lydia E. Pinkham Medicine Company Records, Schlesinger Library, Radcliffe Institute, Harvard University.

While surgery had vastly improved since the early days of the Vegetable Compound, there still existed a strong desire to avoid the practice, where possible. The above portion of an ad produced between 1920 and 1923 is part of a testimonial from two women who claimed to have avoided surgery by using the Vegetable Compound. "Escaped an Operation," *Advertisements in Periodicals*, Vol. VII, 1920–1923, Lydia E. Pinkham Medicine Company, The Lydia E. Pinkham Medicine Company Records, Schlesinger Library, Radcliffe Institute, Harvard University.

Lydia's grandchildren, Lucy and Marion Pinkham, star in the above trade card. Their father Charles worked very hard to get this 1890 promotional piece just right. Cecil Munsey, "Lydia's Medicine, 130 Years Later," 2003, article found on: http://cecilmunsey.com/index.php?option=com_frontpage&Itemid=1

A poster issued by Arthur Cramp (patent medicine foe) as a form of backlash against the Lydia E. Pinkham Company. Cramp wanted to show how the compound's label changed as a result of regulation. This poster could be found in the AMA Bureau of Investigation poster catalog, circa 1930. James Harvey Young, "Arthur Cramp: Quackery Foe," Pharmacy in History, American Institute of the History of Pharmacy (1995), vol. 37, no. 4, 180.

7

In Death, Lydia Still Lights the Way

Through sheer determination, Lydia and sons Dan and Will put the Vegetable Compound on the road to success. Although none lived to see it, in time the remedy's growing popularity would help the extended Pinkham family amass a small fortune. Up to this point, advertising, and lots of it, was a key part of the equation, with promotions + willpower + Lydia's personal touch equaling potion sales. In the years after her death, events conspired to disrupt advertising expenditures, which very likely would have doomed any other patent medicine, but not the compound. A curious thing happened to Lydia's name and image after her passing—both grew larger in death than in life.

When Lydia passed away in May 1883, the business was grossing just under $300,000 a year, with well more than half that spent on advertising. Then, for a period of years, the company hung on to much of its revenue instead of allotting it to advertising, as Charles fended off efforts by ad agent H. P. Hubbard to snatch control of the company.[1]

Once spending resumed over the course of mid- to late-1880s—very slowly at first before revving to full throttle under Hubbard's replacement—another issue arose. After 1883, advertisements were purposely vague because women no longer were writing to Lydia but to her daughter-in-law, Jennie Barker Pinkham. Many still believed they were writing to the original Mrs. Pinkham, and although as the years progressed the company would do less and less to dissuade them of that notion, after Lydia's death an illustration in promotions showed the transition of Jennie taking over her mother-in-law's work. The caption read: "LYDIA E. PINKHAM TO MRS. CHAS. H. PINKHAM: 'My daughter [actually daughter-in-law], you have spent many years of your life in aiding me to compile these records. An analysis of every case of female disease ever brought to my attention is here; this will aid you in perpetuating my work.'"[2]

Newspapers continued to create numerous stories about Lydia as if she were still alive. Her image became an even more familiar sight, not only through the large number of ads, but also from the ongoing coverage she received around the country. The constant flow of articles with information about her background and about the compound soon made her a popular culture figure whose magnitude seemed to build day by day.

Lydia's portrait often served as a comparison point. In 1883, *The Plain Dealer* (Cleveland) described the "Goddess of Liberty" on the new five-cent piece with this compliment: "The Goddess of Liberty is very pretty, and wears a patent medicine smile almost as soothing as that of the famous Lydia Pinkham."[3] That same year, *The Times-Picayune* (New Orleans) called her the "Venus de Medicine,"[4] and in 1901, *The Anaconda Standard* even likened Lydia's image to Queen Victoria's.[5] A dozen years later, the *Kalamazoo Gazette* compared her to the *Mona Lisa*: "So far as real beauty was concerned she never had a thing on Lydia Pinkham."[6]

Not all references were positive. An article in the *Cincinnati Commercial Tribune* blamed Lydia for the rise in suicides and insanity.[7] Advertisements appeared so frequently that the *New Haven Register* noted their rare absences: "The benignant simper of Mrs. Lydia Pinkham has retired from our columns. Lydia must renew her advertisement if she wishes sweet things said of her in Connecticut."[8] Although many people had seen her portrait, an air of mystery shrouded Lydia because few had seen her in person, leaving one writer to assert, "It is said the real Lydia E. Pinkham is a baldheaded chap with red whiskers."[9]

These aspersions aside, even some of her phrases were deemed worthy of adopting. The Women's Athletic Club of Chicago used "Yours for health,"[10] while in 1891 the *Jackson Citizen Patriot* grabbed "Woman sympathizes with woman" to describe Mrs. Frank Leslie's plan to help women after the latter had succeeded her husband as publisher of *Frank Leslie's Illustrated Newspaper*.[11]

Lydia's acclaim also generated its share of rumors and falsehoods, such as in 1883 when *Texas Siftings* magazine reported that she was to be engaged to Sammy Tilden (former governor of New York and 1876 presidential candidate).[12] In 1894, the *American Nonconformist* reported that Bill Nye (a writer and comic of the day) was to be married to Lydia, leading him to joke, "The gay and giddy Lydia had overcome him by her fetching squint and cross-eyed leer and then threw him overboard for a handsomer man."[13] In yet another made-for-gossip romance, when a friend of writer Edward Bok falsely said the latter had married Lydia, Bok received numerous congratulatory letters, to which he responded, "How can I marry a girl who doesn't exist?" (Lydia had died ten years earlier).[14]

The constant barrage of ads with her image angered some consumers. T. G. Scott pleaded in a letter, "Can't you in mercy to the nation have a different [portrait] taken once in a while? Do your hair a little different, say—have a different turn to your head and look solemn. Anything to get rid of that cast-iron smile. . . . You ought to feel solemn anyway, to think that your face pervades the mind of the nation like a nightmare."[15]

A further boost to Lydia's iconic status came months after her death when *The Kansas City Times* reported she received a vote for city physician in the Manchester city government election, the article noting, "She is better qualified for the work in question than half the young doctors who get elected."[16] Similarly, *The New York Times* said in November 1934 that she had received two write-in votes for governor, the ballots cast in protest of the two dominant parties.[17]

As the Vegetable Compound's popularity spread, those who used it sometimes were the butt of jokes, the women often cast as being sick and weak as well as ignorant. In one, a young girl said, "Oh dear! I dropped my bottle of Lydia Pinkham's!" The girl's mother replied, "Aha! A compound fracture!"[18]

Through the jokes, the hyperbole, and even through Lydia's death, the company's ad message never steered far from several points, and perhaps that consistency holds the key to the compound's long-running success. By appealing woman to woman, chiefly through a steady stream of embellished testimonials, the promotions stayed on point and on target. A pitch from June 12, 1883, emphasized how the Vegetable Compound served as a "Medicine for a Woman. Invented by a Woman. Prepared by a Woman." In the text, the compound claimed to be the "Greatest Medical Discovery Since the Dawn of History."[19]

Sometimes, the medicine's very efficacy benefitted advertising. For instance, Emily Field of Kearney, Nebraska, 23, wrote to Lydia about her painful monthly periods. Field then took Lydia's remedy and believed it to be an effective medicine. As a result, the young lady extolled the compound's merits to her father. Later, she wrote to Lydia about advertising in his newspaper, relating, "Having reason to believe your medicine does all that it claims, he has given his consent to my proposition to advertise it if you care to do so." Half the advertising payment was relinquished in favor of medicine for the daughter.[20]

Another key ad message centered on taking action. One advertisement urged, "If the slightest trouble appears which you do not understand write to Mrs. Lydia Pinkham, at Lynn, Mass., for her advice, and a few timely words from her will show you the right thing to do. This advice costs you nothing." Another asserted, "Many a dutiful daughter pays in pain for her mother's ignorance," backed by, "False modesty and procrastination are responsible for much female suffering."[21]

Some ads stretched claims to their limits (and beyond) by saying the remedy revived drooping spirits, invigorated and harmonized organic functions, gave elasticity to the step, restored the natural luster to the eye, and planted on the pale cheek of a woman the fresh roses of life's spring and early summertime. But that was just for starters because the potion also "removes faintness, flatulency, destroys all craving for stimulants, and relieves weakness of the stomach. That feeling of bearing down, causing pain, weight and backache is often permanently cured by its use. It will, at all times and under all circumstances, act in harmony with the laws that govern the system for the cure of Kidney Complaints of either sex." For these reasons, the compound was "unsurpassed."[22]

The remedy also had few peers when it came to bringing in the money. Revenue piled up for Lydia's heirs through the end of the century and beyond, with Charles in particular emerging as an important citizen in Lynn through his wealth. He had married Jennie Barker Jones in 1878 and later become a park commissioner, National City Bank director, and supporter of schools and the hospital.[23] In addition to generous donations to the community, Charles advanced his own interests and pursued his own passions. In the winter he would ride his horses in the snow on Ocean Street and race them in the summer at Readville, Massachusetts, and Franklin Park, among other tracks. He often would relax with a cigar at his favorite club and proved to be a happy individual, leading some to remark, "He has succeeded as he deserved."[24]

A noteworthy figure, Charles often was sought after by reporters. A *Boston Globe* writer asked him, "Fortune, I trust, has attended your efforts?" Charles replied simply, "Yes, we have made some money, if that is what you mean." The reporter responded, "The fact of your not advertising during the last few years is not attributable to a lack of success in your business, as certain parties would have it appear?" Charles retorted,

> I am sincerely glad you asked me that question, as it gives me an opportunity to record a positive refutation of it. Our business has succeeded from the beginning. We dropped out for a while, but we have come to the conclusion that newspaper advertising and our business go hand-in-hand. Therefore, for the past 18 months we have been at it again harder than ever. Oh, we believe in advertising there is nothing like it! Goodbye, sir. Call again.[25]

He was not alone in his comfort. In January 1882, four months before Lydia died, Aroline had married Will Gove and moved to Salem, where her husband had established a successful law practice. He played an important role in the Lydia Pinkham Company in regard to legal matters, and his authority would continue to grow. The Goves built an impressive house on Lafayette Street in Salem.

Charles, Aroline, and Gove replaced Lydia, Dan, and Will on the company's board of directors. On August 21, 1883, they conducted their first meeting, and on January 3, 1884, a second, but the board would not meet again for another 12 years, as Charles managed the company's affairs. He paid off debts and generated million-dollar sales volumes annually, a profit that would allow the Pinkhams and the Goves to accumulate more wealth. But even as the money rolled in, a feud was simmering just beneath the surface that eventually would tear at the families for years to come.[26]

For now, life was good, and the company's first dividends were distributed in 1885. Seeking a creative way to give his sister her earnings, at Thanksgiving dinner Charles made sure Aroline opened a special napkin. When she did, a certified check for $6,000 (nearly $150,000 adjusted for inflation) from her brother fell to the floor. In another show of wealth, he decided to build a sizable mansion on Western Avenue in Lynn, only a block from the patent medicine plant. The grounds became noted for their acres of landscaping, featuring countless trees, dazzling gardens, and a grand telescope. The site played host to many parties that supported such causes as Boston's Woman's Christian Temperance Union (WCTU).[27]

Even before Lydia's death, demand for the compound had prompted the first manufacturing expansion when her cellar kitchen became too small. As a result, the two-story house next door was remodeled as a factory, and the entire operation evolved into a business that aimed at mass-producing the medicine. A staff was hired because Lydia could no longer do it alone.

By 1886, although manufacturing operations had grown, they could not keep pace with consumer cravings. Charles decided it was time to build a bigger plant, referred to by the Pinkhams as a laboratory, to accommodate future growth. Equipment also was enlarged, with macerating jars (for infusing) going from two gallons to thirty gallons and percolators from four gallons to fifty gallons. Over the next ten years, the facility had to be expanded to four times its original size.

With everything inside sterilized, the plant was a model of cleanliness and efficiency, drawing thousands of captivated visitors on tours. This invitation, "PUBLIC INSPECTION INVITED FROM 8 A.M. TO 4 P.M, SATURDAYS AND SUNDAYS EXPECTED," was posted on a factory sign. It also appeared on a series of postcards.[28] Once, a party of four driving to Salem stopped for a visit. The group first viewed the office area filled with typewriters and adding machines, the latest in technology of the day. A superintendent then directed them to the herb room, where multiple bags were stacked. He told the group,

> All our medicines are purely vegetable-made from the roots and herbs and seeds, and in this room all these are stored till used. Some of them come from the fields, woods and gardens of New England, some from other parts of the country, and some from other countries. Many tons of these are used every year in our Laboratory, and you may imagine how much work this means for the collectors who gather them, and for the skilled workers who pick them over. None, but the choicest materials are accepted.[29]

An excerpt from a Boston newspaper marveled,

> In the new Lydia Pinkham laboratory at Lynn, Mass., Chas. H. Pinkham, the general manager, will install an endless chain plant of his own contriving, which will seize the boxes, carry them through the packing room and deliver them through a spout ready for shipping. What amazes a visitor to the works is the numberless stone jars, each with its apron of white rubber cloth, holding the famous compound in process of maceration.[30]

The operation was organized into departments, with a man or a woman standing at each division's helm. The working atmosphere inside the plant was described as "happy," with workers drawing comparatively high wages, bonuses, and other amenities. The personnel addressed Charles casually, calling him Charlie, because the older employees had known him as a child. The Lydia Pinkham Company always remained family oriented, and many who worked in the factory were related in some manner.[31]

At the company's peak in 1925, more than 450 people were employed in the plant. Quite often, the personnel would span generations, and many thought that their job would be a lifelong career. Charles once said, "When you needed to hire somebody, there was always an employee's relative available, so in they came. We never fired anybody or laid them off. When times were slow, we just slowed down the production line."[32]

The personal connection, of course, went beyond the workplace and right back to Lydia, whose legacy would continue to be a driving force during the tough years that were to come. An article in the *Daily Inter Ocean* (Chicago) in 1894 told of a Pinkham employee who worked as a company correspondent. The worker would always use Lydia's signature when replying to letters despite the fact that Mrs. Pinkham had been dead for more than ten years. The *Inter Ocean* even claimed that the correspondent, before going to bed, would utter this prayer: "For thine is the kingdom and the power and the glory forever and ever. Amen, Yours for health. Lydia"[33]

NOTES

1. Jean Burton, *Lydia Pinkham Is Her Name* (New York: Little and Ives, 1949), 208–9; Charles H. Pinkham, "Advertising 1875–1953," 1953, 36-38, The Lydia E. Pinkham Medicine Company Records, Schlesinger Library, Radcliffe Institute, Harvard University; and Cecil Munsey, "Lydia's Medicine, 130 Years Later," *CecilMunsey.com*, 2003, http://cecilmunsey.com/index.php?option=com_docman&task=doc_download&gid=788&&Itemid=34.

2. "A Life's Experience," *Lippincott's Monthly Magazine* (November 1892): 711.

3. "News in Brief," *Plain Dealer* (Cleveland, OH), vol. 39, no. 28, February 1, 1883.

4. [No Title], *Times-Picayune*, published as the *Daily Picayune* (New Orleans, LA), April 15, 1883, 16, col. 1.

5. [No Title], *Anaconda Standard* (Anaconda, MT), vol. 12, no. 139, January 27, 1901, 6.

6. Roy K. Moulton, "Moulton Lead from the Editor's Pencil," *Kalamazoo Gazette* (Kalamazoo, MI), March 4, 1914, 5.

7. Kate Sanborn, "Smith College," *Cincinnati Commercial Tribune*, published as the *Cincinnati Commercial*, vol. 42, no. 91, December 25, 1881, 1.

8. "Persons and Things," *New Haven Register*, published as *New Haven Evening Register* (New Haven, CT), vol. 42, no. 52, March 3, 1882, 2.

9. [No Title], *Times-Picayune*, November 2, 1882, 4.

10. [No Title], *Sunday Herald* (Boston), May 28, 1899, 16, col. 6.

11. "Woman's World: Mrs. Frank Leslie's Scheme to Help Women Who Need It," *Jackson Citizen Patriot* (Jackson, MI), March 26, 1891, 6.

12. [No Title], *Texas Siftings* (Austin, TX), vol. 3, no. 7, June 23, 1883, 1.

13. [No Title], *American Nonconformist* (Indianapolis, IN), no. 740, August 30, 1894, 4.

14. "Book Chat," *Themis* (Sacramento, CA), vol. 4, no. 39, November 12, 1892, 3.

15. T. G. Scott to Mrs. Lydia E. Pinkham, March 30, 1880, letter in Elysa Ream Engelman, "'The Face That Haunts Me Ever': Consumers, Retailers, Critics, and the Branded Personality of Lydia E. Pinkham" (PhD diss., Boston University, 2003), 167–68.

16. [No Title], *Kansas City Times* (Kansas City, MO), February 6, 1885, 4.

17. "Voted for Lydia Pinkham," *New York Times*, November 23, 1934, 40, cited in Engelman, "Face That Haunts Me".

18. The joke about Lydia Pinkham is of uncertain origin, but likely began and spread by word of mouth, Engelman, "Face That Haunts Me," 186.

19. "Lydia E. Pinkham's Vegetable Compound Is a Positive Cure," *Michigan Farmer*, June 12, 1883, 3.

20. Emily N. Fields to Lydia E. Pinkham, February 24, 1881, Box 167 Folder 3113, The Lydia E. Pinkham Medicine Company Records, Schlesinger Library, Radcliffe Institute, Harvard University, quoted in Engelman, "Face That Haunts Me," 14.

21. "I Hate to ask my Doctor," *San Francisco Call*, Vol. 70, 48, July 18, 1891; "Indulge in Mothers," *Sacramento Daily Union*, Vol. 97, 72, May 4, 1899; and *The Sacred Heart Review*, Vol. 29, 2, January 10, 1903.

22. "A Medicine for a Woman. Invented by a Woman. Prepared by a Woman," *Youth's Companion* 55, no. 41, (October 12, 1882): 412, col. 4.

23. Burton, *Lydia Pinkham*, 210–211; Charles H. Pinkham and Jennie B. Jones, marriage registration no. 206 (September 11, 1887), *Marriages Registered in the City of Lynn, for the Year 1878, Massachusetts Vital Records, 1840–1915, Marriages 1878*, 223, Ancestry.com, *Massachusetts, Marriage Records, 1840–1915* [online database] (Provo, UT: Ancestry.com Operations, 2013). Original Data: *Massachusetts Vital Records, 1840–1911* (Boston: New England Historic Genealogical Society); and *Massachusetts Vital Records, 1911–1915* (Boston: New England Historic Genealogical Society), http://search.ancestry.com/search/db.aspx?dbid=2511.

24. Burton, *Lydia Pinkham*, 210-211

25. Ibid., 223–24.

26. C. H. Pinkham, "Advertising 1875–1953," 105–6, The Lydia E. Pinkham Medicine Company Records, Schlesinger Library, Radcliffe Institute, Harvard University.

27. Burton, *Lydia Pinkham*, 209–10; Sarah Stage, *Female Complaints: Lydia Pinkham and the Business of Women's Medicine* (New York: Norton, 1979), 167–68; and "Inflation Calculator," Dave Manuel.com, http://www.davemanuel.com/inflation-calculator.php.

28. Burton, *Lydia Pinkham*, 113–14, 211–12; and "The Come and See Sign," *Michigan Farmer* 53, no. 17 (April 25, 1908): 448.

29. "How We Visited the Laboratory" (1908), 1, 5 [unpaginated] in file "The Lydia E. Pinkham Plant, History of Mfg. Process," MC 181, 2635, The Lydia E. Pinkham Medicine Company Records, Schlesinger Library, Radcliffe Institute, Harvard University.

30. Burton, *Lydia Pinkham*, 211–12.

31. Ibid., 212–213; and Edward J. Julian, "Lydia Pinkham's Legacy," *Pictorial Living Magazine, Boston Sunday Herald Advertiser*, June 16, 1974, 8, 10, 12, in vertical files of the Lynn (MA) Public Library, s.v. Biographies and Obituaries, Pinkham, Lydia.

32. Dan Yaeger, "The Lady Who Helped Ladies," *Yankee* 53, no. 9 (September 1989): 116; and Munsey, "Lydia's Medicine."

33. "Intellectual Habit: Petition of an Employee in a Certain Medicine Company," *Inter Ocean*, published as the *Daily Inter Ocean* (Chicago, IL), vol. 22, no. 287, January 7, 1894, 27.

8

The 1890s

Years of Triumph and Turmoil

As the Lydia E. Pinkham Medicine Company prepared to close the books on the nineteenth century, a new ad agent was in place, Charles was in charge, and American women could not get enough of the Vegetable Compound.

For years the company reached its target audience by relying on images of happiness and health, presumably achieved by customers consuming its products. But as Victorian shackles slowly gave way to progressive ideals, new methods emerged to connect with women as they boldly stepped out of the shadows and into the workforce. In a subtle but strategic shift, powerful images were added to the advertising mix depicting a darker side of life, including women being fired or collapsing from overwork in the home or in a factory.[1] The message was that whether the issue was "female troubles" or job fatigue, the compound and the company's other products would give women the strength to take on a changing world.

While instilling the customer base with a shot of health-giving confidence, the campaign's success also entrenched the Vegetable Compound as a household name and brought the Pinkham Company ten years of financial prosperity.[2] But the good times weren't all good, and because the period also was marked by ongoing battles with counterfeiters and years consumed in a family power struggle, by the end of the decade, it would be the company that needed to be healed.

For better or worse, the Pinkhams' fortunes were tied to ad agent James T. Wetherald, a young ex-newspaper writer who in 1889 had replaced the combative H. P. Hubbard.[3] The latter had exited after a stormy ten-year reign in which he ingratiated himself with the family through his marketing wizardry, only to lose favor with an unsuccessful bid to take control of the company. A key early issue for Wetherald was convincing potential customers in the early 1890s that Lydia Pinkham actually ever existed. She had been dead for years, and Wetherald wanted to bring her back to life figuratively by updating her portrait and conveying that letters to her were being answered without interruption. Although Charles initially vetoed the idea, the agent persevered, and this paragraph was added to the promotions: "Lydia Pinkham's private letters from ladies in all parts of the world average one hundred per day, and truly she has been a mother to the race. Suffering women ever seek her in their extremity, and find both a helper and a friend. Correspondents will receive prompt and conscientious answers, and the sympathy of a mother.[4]

The matter demanded attention because newspapers, the company's chief advertising vehicle, and letter writers were starting to ask uncomfortable questions, such as this example in 1895 from a Seattle publication:

> But of all the bare-faced frauds commend me to the Lydia Pinkham ads. Now this very nice old lady died upwards of ten years ago. Yet to this day respectable women . . . write letters to Lydia Pinkham and tell how one bottle of her nostrum saved their lives and how they now feel like new women, and go into details of female irregularities with a shocking disregard to the proprieties! When one stops to consider that Lydia Pinkham is long since dead and left no children, nor any recipes of her valuable female lotions, it would appear as though someone is working the old lady's name for all there is in it.[5]

Or this one in a letter from Chattanooga, Tennessee: "You doubtless are not aware that I know old 'Mrs. Lydia' is a young quack of the male sex. This fact is more widely known Mr. Lydia than you have any idea."[6]

Charles addressed some of the rumors on a stop in Chicago on his way to the West for a vacation. In an 1896 interview with the *Chicago Times-Herald*, he asserted, "Of course, the mere idea is absurd to me, her son, who knew her to be the kindest, sweetest, gentlest mother in the world. She was all her portrait speaks her to be, and her whole life was given up to doing all the good she could in this weary world. I am proud to say that my mother was not a myth and that there was not a drop of selfishness in her makeup."[7]

With the new ad campaign, Wetherald rationalized that he was not stretching truth but rather portraying everyday aspects of Lydia's life. Whatever the case, Charles eventually bought in and decided the *Boston Herald* would be the company's chief ad outlet, although he still wanted to test the agent's effectiveness. At the end of March 1890, Charles wrote to the agency,

> I am beginning to feel a little good result from the *Herald* [advertising], just enough to know it is beginning to count. Of course I can't tell to what extent. But enough for me to feel justified in appropriating $1,000 more to be used according to your judgment in the *Boston Journal*, say every other day. And, if you think best, in the *Sunday Globe*.[8]

When sales increased in May, Charles authorized advertising in New Hampshire, Maine, and Vermont. By July, he upped the amount to $40,000 and by winter had extended the program to Illinois, Indiana, Minnesota, Iowa, Wisconsin, Missouri, and California.[9]

Regardless of the campaign, Wetherald insisted on these "musts" for every ad:

- Product name. The words "Lydia E. Pinkham's Vegetable Compound" must appear in bold type. Many women have forgotten the remedy; others have never heard of it. They must be made to see it and remember it.
- Trade-mark. Most women don't know what Mrs. Pinkham looked like. Too many don't believe she ever lived. This situation must be remedied.
- Bill-of-fare. Women must be told again and again what the product will do. Every trouble that a woman has which can be cured by the Comp. should be listed and the women assured that the Comp. is a positive cure for such trouble. (J. T. always referred to such a listing of symptoms as the "bill of fare.")
- Guide to Health and Etiquette. We should rewrite the Company's pamphlet "Guide to Health" and offer to mail it out. If a woman is healthy when she reads Comp. [advertising] she won't write for a booklet that just tells her how to keep well; but every woman wants to learn more about etiquette. And the new name will add tone to the Comp. We should call it an illustrated book and say that it was written by Lydia E. Pinkham. Women will think they are getting something of more value if we make them send in two 2-cent stamps.
- Orders by mail. If a woman can't buy the Comp. from her druggist, she should be able to buy it direct from the Company. This statement should be included in every ad: "All druggists sell it as a standard article, or sent by mail, in form of Pills or Lozenges, on receipt of $1.00."[10]

After maneuvering through the "Lydia lived" minefield, the company courted controversy again over the issue of birth control and douching. By the late nineteenth century, it was common for women to douche to avoid pregnancy, after Dr. Charles Knowlton had recommended the practice years earlier in his groundbreaking work on birth control, *Fruits of Philosophy*. Because douching also was considered a legitimate hygienic and therapeutic practice based on the advice of Lydia Pinkham and others, women were able to supplement the process by buying a device not sold exclusively for contraceptive purposes. That was important because Comstock Laws of the time prohibited the sale of contraceptive devices. The Pinkhams avoided prosecution by including in ads for their Sanative Wash a referral for Ruth Paxton's "Improved Fountain Syringe," available by mail for $1.50. However, the Paxton Company existed only on paper, allowing the Pinkham Company to profit off sales of both the douche and the syringe.[11]

Lydia's advocacy issues aside, testimonials were the foundation of the company's ad campaigns, and by the end of 1884, Wetherald had parlayed them into a 45-percent boost in sales.[12] Over the years, Charles and Wetherald experimented with advertising in many types of media but generally held to the practice of directing 90 percent of ad spending to newspapers. The agent said of his strategy,

> Except for the booklets, we confine all of the Pinkham advertising to newspapers, because we think they are best fitted for what we are seeking to do. Street cars and outdoor signs are doubtless all very good for advertising some kinds of goods, but for

our business I do not consider them favorably. We have to tell more of a story than we can get on a card or a billboard, and we have to back it up with testimonials. Frequency of issue is a great feature, for it allows us to tell more and varied stories and to multiply testimonials. Therefore, I rank the daily papers first, the weeklies next, and the monthly last. And I am inclined to prefer the evening daily over the morning, for it goes into the homes more and is, I think, more thoroughly read.[13]

Charles was amassing great wealth, and other Pinkhams and the Goves were getting rich in the midst of record-breaking sales. Perils posed by counterfeiters and others would surface all too soon, but generally all was right in the world until 1900, when out of nowhere everything changed, and the Pinkhams and Goves would be at war over control of the company.

On November 10, at age 56, Charles died while battling kidney disease. Employees mourned, and the family and much of the nation mourned with them, as noted in this obituary: "From an exceedingly small beginning the largest business in the proprietary medicine line in the United States was built. Under his management the industry prospered, until now more than 400 employees are left who revere and honor his name. Mr. Pinkham had no more devoted friends than those whom he employed."[14]

Even as condolences poured in, a power struggle was taking shape, and changes were afoot that would define the company for the next five decades. Soon after Charles's passing, Aroline called a board-of-directors meeting at which she intended to see her husband elected president.[15] After Will Gove was elected president, he was given the additional power to run the company as general manager: "It was unanimously voted that until otherwise ordered said William H. Gove have power to act for the directors and company so far as is not inconsistent with law or the by-laws of the company in all cases in which in his opinion the whole board cannot conveniently act."[16] As the Goves consolidated authority, troubles mounted for the Pinkham family, which found itself without a spot on the board. But counterfeiters posed a more immediate threat to the company, and they would command everyone's attention.

Not long before Charles died, he was working with Pinkerton detectives and the police to track down forgers who would either steal bottles of patent medicines or duplicate them and then fill the containers with cheap concoctions, such as stale beer, for resale. Phony bottles of Vegetable Compounds were unloaded on unsuspecting druggists, and soon a flourishing trade was established. In early 1900, a druggist in Scranton, Pennsylvania, alerted authorities to a man named Howells, who was passing off bogus bottles of the compound and other patent medicines. Charles shared investigation expenses with other company owners, and within three months, detectives found Howells in Cleveland. The Dauphin County Court ruled that Howells was guilty of counterfeiting, fined him $350, and ordered him to spend eighteen months in jail.[17] The Pinkhams spent $7,324.20 for the detectives, and although their efforts stopped a counterfeiter, the problem didn't go away.[18]

Laws at the time were not as effective at combatting fakes as they are today, which encouraged many copycats to sell their bogus products at just about any store.[19] Counterfeit compounds not only hurt sales but also put consumers at risk because several of the dangerous mixtures made people sick or worse. Fears about the Vegetable Compound rose among some consumers, driving them to other remedies.[20]

The Pinkham Company put some of blame on certain druggists who it said would go outside regular distribution lines to make their purchases at a discount. Pharmacists eventually formed the National Association of Retail Druggists (NARD), whose members agreed not to buy from price-cutters and who would share information about suspicious individuals.[21] The Pinkham Company and more than sixty other manufacturers also signed the NARD plan, pledging not to sell products to price-cutters.[22] Through these and other efforts, the problem of counterfeiting largely went away domestically, although it would crop back up in the late 1930s in foreign markets where different rules and regulations made prosecutions more difficult.[23]

As the counterfeit crisis ebbed, the industry was spending unheard amounts of money on advertising. At one point after the turn of the century, the Pinkham Company was allocating $800,000 a year for newspaper spots, at the time the largest appropriation ever by a patent medicine company.[24] The industry's spending may have coaxed other advertisers to join in the spree, with the National Biscuit Company rolling out the first million-dollar campaign shortly thereafter.[25]

By 1904, the good times convinced Wetherald to break away from the Pettingill agency and form his own outfit in Boston, James T. Wetherald Advertising.[26] In addition to the Pinkham account, he advertised his own merchandise, Sykes Comfort Powder, and such products as the Fountain Syringe and Paxtine Douche Tablets from the Pinkhams' shell company, Ruth Paxton. With these "clients," James T. Wetherald Advertising was recognized as a legitimate agency, qualifying it to place ads.[27]

Nearly everyone and everything involved with the company seemed to be gaining traction except the Pinkham family. Without a spot on the board and with few legal avenues to pursue, the Pinkhams watched as the Goves pretty much ran things. A number of employees loyal to the Pinkhams had been discharged, and tensions in offices and at the plant were growing daily.[28] Esther Gove, a relative of Aroline, had allegiances on both sides of the feud: "You didn't know whether to satisfy the Pinkhams or the Goves. If you were in the middle of the line, you were all right, but everyone stayed tight-lipped."[29]

The great equalizer turned out to be Arthur, Charles's eldest son, who studied at Brown University at the turn of the century and, much to everyone's surprise, had managed to learn a great deal about the inner workings of the company. In a premed course, he soaked up knowledge about medicine, while in another he calculated alcohol's outsized expense as a compound ingredient and later convinced his father to purchase a still that within two years helped recover $50,000 worth of alcohol.[30]

Arthur also learned how to manufacture the Vegetable Compound, and after abandoning plans to go Harvard Medical School so he could comfort his stressed-out mother when Charles died, he set up a factory in one of his mother's buildings. Arthur was able to produce a potion indistinguishable from the Vegetable Compound, and because neither the ingredients nor the manufacturing process was patented, he was ready for a fight, declaring, "We're going into competition with the Lydia E. Pinkham Medicine Company."[31] Considering that the compound's label was trademarked, he used his popular father's picture instead for his product and called it the Delmac Vegetable Compound (representing the first letter of his given name and those of his siblings). Some of the discharged Pinkham Company employees were rehired to operate the Delmac Medicine Company, and in early 1901, the first full-page Delmac ad appeared in the *Lynn Daily Evening Item*, claiming that the new product would be available in drugstores.[32]

Delmac also seemed to have Lydia Pinkham's seal of approval, with this announcement inserted into the packaging:

Mrs. Pinkham of the Lydia E. Pinkham Medicine Company of Lynn, Mass., sends this letter and gives us permission to publish it. . .

The Delmac Medicine Company Lynn, Mass.,

I am very much pleased with your Liver Regulator—Delmac.

I have seen its curative value so well demonstrated in a number of severe cases that I am convinced it is an excellent medicine.

Recently a very miraculous cure which it had effected was brought to my attention.

Wishing you every success,

Yours for Health,
/s/ [signed] Mrs. Pinkham[33]

In February 1901, in a final bit of brinksmanship, Arthur met with Will Gove and laid out his plan. After asking Gove to examine the new product and taste it, Arthur presented the advertising campaign Wetherald had produced and showed Gove a letter from the Lynn Postmaster in which the latter agreed to deliver all mail addressed to "Mrs. Pinkham Lynn, Mass." to Mrs. Charles H. Pinkham.[34]

Arthur's strategy must have had its desired effect because on March 2, Aroline, Will Gove, Jennie B. Pinkham (Charles's widow), and Arthur signed two agreements. The first said the Pinkham family would not make competing products, while the second named Jennie the director and manager of the private letter department and Arthur the company vice president and secretary. Both got seats on the board, and Arthur was put in charge of foreign trade, advertising, and the creation of the medicine. Employees who had been discharged were reinstated, and the latest round of harmony found Will Gove and Arthur working together on key initiatives. Foremost was the brand's push into foreign markets, an endeavor that would test not only the company's resolve but also the new bond between the two families.[35]

As early as 1882, the Lydia Pinkham Company was selling products in Canada and sections of South America, but almost another twenty years would pass before the firm ventured into overseas shores and tested distant markets once again.[36] From England to China, Cuba to Holland, and at ports in between, the Vegetable Compound was introduced to new customers in fits and starts from the early 1900s through the 1920s. In a few countries, products were sold well into the 1950s.

There were some successes—Panama and parts of the Caribbean—but mostly there was disappointment because, despite the ambition and good intentions, the effort to establish the brand abroad fell victim to poor preparation, poor execution, and the fact the company was probably stretched too thin to pull it off.[37] Its foray into Britain, for example, generated steady sales but at too great a cost. In their postmortem, company executives bemoaned the fact that annual advertising expenditures were only $16,000 for a country that size. Also, test campaigns should have been conducted in representative cities and the ad copy altered accordingly. The biggest mistake, however, was in regarding Britain as one market rather than a group of markets.[38]

The latter mistake was made time and again, country after country. World War I interrupted some efforts, but perhaps Will Gove got to the heart of the problem when he told ad agents from China, Japan, and Russia, "We are not yet ready to put our goods on sale in your country."[39] The Pinkham Company had gotten a little ahead of itself and paid the price. But following Lydia's lead, the firm was never afraid of being out front, sometimes to its detriment more often to its credit. It's what pioneers of any age do.

NOTES

1. Charles H. Pinkham, "Advertising 1875–1953," 1953, 117, The Lydia E. Pinkham Medicine Company Records, Schlesinger Library, Radcliffe Institute, Harvard University; and Elizabeth V. Burt, "From 'True Woman' to 'New Woman,'" *Journalism History* 37, no. 4 (Winter 2012): 210–11.

2. C. H. Pinkham, "Advertising 1875–1953," 119.

3. Ibid., 74.

4. Ibid., 80.

5. Jean Burton, *Lydia Pinkham Is Her Name* (New York: Little and Ives, 1949), 221–222.

6. Ibid., 222.

7. "Tribute to a Mother Interview with Charles H. Pinkham: Malicious Stories about Lydia E. Pinkham," *Ohio Farmer (1856–1906)* 89, no 20 (May 14, 1896): 424.

8. C. H. Pinkham, "Advertising 1875–1953," 74.

9. Ibid., 74–75.

10. Ibid., 76–77.

11. Charles Knowlton, *Fruits of Philosophy: An Essay on the Population Question* (London: Free Thought, [1877]), 73–75.

12. C. H. Pinkham, "Advertising 1875–1953, 86–92." Examples of these ads are on pages 87–92.

13. Ibid., 116.

14. Burton, *Lydia Pinkham*, 230–31; and "Death of Lydia E. Pinkham's Son: Popular Head of Great Business," *Sunday Times-Herald* (Chicago), November 11, 1900, 3, cols. 2-3.

15. C. H. Pinkham, "Advertising 1875–1953," 107–8.

16. Ibid.

17. Ibid., 113–14; and Elysa Ream Engelman, "'The Face That Haunts Me Ever': Consumers, Retailers, Critics, and the Branded Personality of Lydia E. Pinkham" (PhD diss., Boston University, 2003), 88.

18. C. H. Pinkham, "Advertising 1875–1953," 114.

19. Engelman, "Face That Haunts Me," 88; and "Only Sour Beer," *Daily Evening Item* (Lynn, MA), December 21, 1883, 1, col. 5.

20. "Only Sour Beer," 1, col. 5.

21. Engelman, "Face That Haunts Me," 95–96; and E. R. Cooper, Organizer Northern Ohio Druggist Association, "Check on Counterfeit Goods," *The Pharmaceutical Era* (June 14, 1900): 634.

22. Ibid., 95; and "N.A.R.D. Notes," *The Pharmaceutical Era*, January 11, 1900, vol. 23, 50.

23. For the Cuban incident, see Daniel Pinkham to Guy N. F. Ford, April 19, 1938; for the British Honduras case, see correspondence between Nord and Pinkham dated December 7, 1939, and January 11, 1940, box 168, folder 3156, The Lydia E. Pinkham Medicine Company Records, Schlesinger Library, Radcliffe Institute, Harvard University.

24. Burton, *Lydia Pinkham*, 223; and C. H. Pinkham, "Advertising 1875–1953," 126.

25. John McDonough and Karen Egolf, eds., *The Advertising Age Encyclopedia of Advertising*, vol. 3, *P–Z* (New York: Fitzroy Dearborn, 2003), 1597.

26. C. H. Pinkham, "Advertising 1875–1953," 103–4.

27. Ibid., 104.

28. Ibid., 109.

29. Dan Yaeger, "The Lady Who Helped Ladies," *Yankee* 53, no. 9 (September 1989): 116, 118.

30. C. H. Pinkham, "Advertising 1875–1953," 109.

31. Ibid., 110–11.

32. Ibid.

33. Ibid.

34. Ibid.

35. Ibid., 111.

36. Ibid., 46, 132.

37. Ibid., 132, 140–41, 143–44.

38. Ibid., 132–39.

39. Ibid., 132.

9

The Gospel According to Lydia

Whether blazing trails for women or taking on the medical establishment, Lydia Pinkham often was at odds with tradition and convention. Never one to bow to custom, her indomitable spirit inspired the other Pinkhams to follow paths less traveled. Where some companies might rely on flash and dash to promote their products, for many years her enterprise was not afraid to stick to its basic principles. In most testimonials of the day, celebrities and influential figures served as pitchmen, while trade cards as a rule were decorated with humorous or flowery scenes to call attention to this or that commodity.

For the Pinkhams and their Vegetable Compound, endorsements came from everyday women to give potential customers sentiments with which they could more easily relate.[1] The focus was on the product, not the VIP. The words came from real customers in state after state, not from phrases dreamed up in an advertising office. In the company's early ad campaigns, Lydia's ubiquitous portrait was about the only nod to imagery, giving way later to the successful Brooklyn Bridge promotional piece and to bigger changes still by the end of the nineteenth century.

A series of circulars and pamphlets rounded out the Pinkhams' message to women, but Lydia wasn't content to stop there. In the ultimate break with convention, she always envisioned dedicating an entire book to present her blueprint for living a healthy life, which of course included taking daily doses of the compound. She began by writing a pamphlet, "A Guide to Women," which was reissued many times under a variety of titles, with more than 11 million copies in print. Finally, in 1905, well after her death, *Lydia E. Pinkham's Private Text-Book upon Ailments Peculiar to Women* was published based on her advice to women.[2] This contribution to the nation's general welfare, perhaps her crowning achievement, was a compendium not only of the ad campaigns but also of the advice Lydia (and her surrogates) had dispensed through the years that formed the basis of the company's testimonials.

A disquieting aspect of the patent medicine business was its reliance on the placebo effect. The phenomenon, a perceived improvement in a health condition that is not attributable to an actual treatment, was at the heart of the Vegetable Compound's success. Although there is doubt about the remedy's true effectiveness in relieving symptoms of various ailments, there is no question that advertising led tens of thousands of people to believe the concoction actually worked.[3] And many were only too happy to write to the Lydia Pinkham Company and praise the medicine. The testimonials, in turn, became parts of new ads, such as this one from Mrs. Melva Routon of Camby, Indiana:

I have used Lydia E. Pinkham's Vegetable Compound and found it to be of great benefit to me. The doctors said I had womb trouble. I had the headache all the time, also a terrible backache, was nervous, cross and irritable. I looked so pale that people would ask me what was the matter. I suffered in this way for about four years, until one day about in despair my husband brought me a bottle of Lydia E. Pinkham's Vegetable Compound. I commenced its use, and much to every one's surprise, it cured me. It has completely changed my disposition for the better also.[4]

In correspondence, Lydia (and later the company's team of communicators under the direction of daughter-in-law Jennie Barker Pinkham) wasn't shy about touting the compound's capacity to treat everything from signs of sterility to postpartum ailments. These back-and-forths also became fodder for promotions, with one adding support to the other. An ad excerpt in 1898 from Mrs. W. E. Paxton of Youngtown, North Dakota, revealed a common theme in compound advertising regarding troubled pregnancies and how relief was just a swallow away:

After the birth of my little girl, three years ago, my health was very poor; I had leucorrhoea badly, and a terrible bearing-down pain which gradually grew worse, until I could do no work. Also had headache nearly all the time, and dizzy feelings. Menstruations were very profuse, appearing every two weeks. I took medicine from a good doctor, but it seemed to do no good. I was becoming alarmed over my condition, when I read your advertisement in a paper. I sent at once for a bottle of Lydia E. Pinkham's Vegetable Compound, and after taking two-thirds of the bottle I felt so much better that I send for two more. After using three bottles I felt as strong and well as any one.[5]

If the compound was good for what ailed most women, the ads said other Pinkham products in combination were even better for such conditions as inflammation of the ovaries.[6] One ad in 1898 featured a letter from Mrs. Carrie F. Tremper of Lake, Indiana, who dealt with her ovarian troubles by taking three different Pinkham remedies:

I was suffering from congestion of the ovaries, misplacement of the womb, irregular, scanty, and painful menstruation, also kidney trouble. I had let it go on until I could not sit up, and could not straighten my left leg. My physician gave me relief, but failed to cure me. Reading the testimonials of different women, telling what Lydia E. Pinkham's

Vegetable Compound had done for them, I decided to give it a trial. I had almost given up hopes, as I had suffered untold agony. The first dose helped me. And now, after using eight bottles of Vegetable Compound, one bottle of Blood Purifier, one box of Liver Pills, I am proud to say I am as well as I ever was. I might have saved a large doctor's bill and much suffering, had I tried your precious medicine in the beginning of my sickness.[7]

Husbands also were encouraged to get in on the action, instructed in ads that if they had sick wives they should "sit down and write a letter to that friend of women, Mrs. Pinkham, of Lynn, Mass., state fully and freely the whole case to her, and she will honestly advise you what to do." Buy her bottles of the Vegetable Compound, the men were promised, and soon they would see improvements, until their spouses were once again the same women they had first married.[8]

From 1895 to 1935, women who allowed their testimonials to be used in ads were sent presents at Christmastime. The idea came from a Pinkham secretary who wrote to Wetherald,

We have been thinking that it would be a good scheme to get something as a Christmas present for our testimonial women who write so many letters for us, something they could always keep. We think that a silver souvenir spoon would be nice, and could not we get one made for us with Mrs. Pinkham's head on it? It would be a perpetual reminder, and we think they would appreciate it.[9]

By 1898, a yearly order of five hundred spoons was typical.[10] One group of testimonials not appreciated until many years later was from black women. Worried that their inclusion would upset white customers, Wetherald's agency issued this directive: "Enclosed we hand you the testimonial to be used instead of Mrs. Lucy Lerne. You gave me Mrs. Lerne's last week and today we have heard that she is colored. Think you had better use this one in its place." Despite such discrimination, Pinkham products gained a following among black women, and by the 1930s their testimonials and photographs were part of the ad campaigns.[11] Twenty years later, druggists began to refer to middle-aged black women as the "typical" Vegetable Compound user.[12]

If testimonials were the Pinkhams' advertising bread and butter, over time trading cards became their jam, forming a sweet overlay for the company's advertising message. Research by Ellen Gruber Garvey showed that advertisers recognized that women liked to collect the cards and swap information.[13] Kathy Peiss's cultural study of cosmetics coined the phrase *beauty culture*, a phenomenon of beauty parlors and back porches in which women gave one another informal advice about beauty and health.[14]

Although many companies jumped on the trading-card bandwagon, the Pinkhams' initial forays focused on Lydia's portrait, the phrase "Yours for Health," and text promoting the Vegetable Compound.[15] Bland by comparison to others' promotional campaigns, the Pinkhams hung on to their approach for a time until the portrait began to lose its effectiveness. Heeding druggists' requests for more imagery, the company distributed point-of-sale pieces with scenes of coastal landscapes.[16]

By the spring of 1889, Charles wanted to use images of his daughters (Lydia's granddaughters) in the trading cards, which set off a drawn-out process.[17] Charles commissioned Knapp and Company to create an oil painting based on a photograph of the children, ages three and five, then engaged in a months-long dispute over the tiniest details before settling on an image that was used on the cards.[18]

Although trading cards had their place, pamphlets were an advertising mainstay from the company's earliest years. From this platform, Lydia probed deeper into women's roles, often asserting that they were a "slave to drudgery, routine, and the neighbors' watchful scrutiny."[19] She urged women to beware of sacrificing their health while caring for their young, saying they should "preserve their health and lengthen lives of usefulness."[20] From 1893 to 1953, the Pinkhams and Goves distributed 167 multipage booklets. By the turn of the century, the pamphlets also promoted such novelties as sachet perfumes, sold via mail for twenty-five cents, while continuing to cross-promote other Pinkham products, including the Sanative Wash and Fountain Syringe.[21]

In other pamphlets, topics included:

- why experience is the "perfect teacher,"
- how Lydia does what she does,
- what steps are taken to prevent men from reading letters written to Lydia,[22]
- how the compound does what it does[23]
- Lydia's views on the future[24]
- detailed accounts of the reproductive process[25]
- detailed descriptions of women's reproductive organs[26]
- disorders associated with menstruation[27]
- information about other Pinkham products[28]
- disorders associated with pregnancy[29]

During World War I, a pamphlet called the *War Time Cook and Health Book* offered the standard advice and included many of the same promotions. But on a page devoted to serving the country in support of the war, women were directed to eat meats other than beef and pork and to consume cereals other than wheat in order to help conserve these three commodities.[30]

All such efforts served as preludes to the textbook, which was distributed for free and championed Lydia's assertion that the "women of this country must have physical education, if we are to have a people strong and hearty."[31]

As if its *Lydia E. Pinkham's Private Text-Book upon Ailments Peculiar to Women* title weren't warning enough about its contents, an early "Caution to the Owner" note says, "This little book treats of delicate subjects, and has been sent to you only by request. It is not intended for indiscriminate reading, but for your own private information."[32] The first chapter explores differences between the sexes, the virtues and pitfalls of motherhood, the risks of surgery, and the wonders of Lydia and her compound. Subsequent chapters

- examine mothers' crucial role in society and scorn women who choose not to bear children: "The charge that women do not wish to become mothers is one of the greatest of many gross and unfair libels which women have had to endure in silence. They are the few and unnatural who would not prefer this normal privilege of womankind";[33]
- impart detailed information about menstruation, including the hardships and myths: "The average woman with true modesty refrains from making her troubles known, where often a kind heart would be only too ready to relieve her of many of her burdens," the book advises, while also noting the positive effects of the Vegetable Compound;[34]
- champion the compound's capacity for dealing with everything from the "change of life" to tumors.[35] In regard to the latter, the book advises, somewhat shockingly, that they are "often dissolved and expelled when early discovered if proper treatment is adopted" but also makes the rare admission that "when the tumor has been allowed to become extremely large, it may be that nothing but surgical treatment will be effective."[36]
- stretch credibility when reviewing such conditions as obesity, for which the textbook lists anemia as a cause.[37]

Although the book enjoyed lasting popularity, the other forms of advertising eventually ran their courses. But before they did, there was no doubting their impact on the bottom line and on the Pinkhams' legacy. From 1889 to 1898, for instance, sales increased 2,500 percent on ad expenditures of 49 percent of total sales. The total profit equaled 24 percent of the sales, numbers that made it hard to deny the advertising was effective. But by the end of that period, Charles and Wetherald wondered whether the business had reached its saturation point in terms of advertising. So in 1899, ad expenditures were reduced to assess the effect on the sales volumes, which also decreased.[38] Armed with these figures, Wetherald persuaded the company to increase ad spending by 28 percent in 1903, to $843,608, which was $57,000 more than had ever been spent in a single year. Despite the massive outlay, sales rose only one-half of 1 percent, prompting Wetherald to admit that his advertising was losing its appeal.[39]

The timing could not have been worse for him or the company because they were about to face an onslaught that would forever change the direction of the patent medicine industry.

NOTES

1. For examples of Lydia Pinkham testimonial ads, see *Advertisements in Periodicals*, vol. 1, *1890–1900*, The Lydia E. Pinkham Medicine Company Records, Schlesinger Library, Radcliffe Institute, Harvard University.

2. Dan Yaeger, "The Lady Who Helped Ladies," *Yankee* 53, no. 9 (September 1989): 67; and *Lydia E. Pinkham's Private Text-Book upon Ailments Peculiar to Women* (Lynn, MA: Lydia Pinkham Medicine, 1905).

3. Elysa Ream Engelman, "'The Face That Haunts Me Ever': Consumers, Retailers, Critics, and the Branded Personality of Lydia E. Pinkham" (PhD diss., Boston University, 2003), 53.

4. "Wise Advice to Husbands," *Massachusetts Ploughman and New England Journal of Agriculture* 56, no. 27 (April 3, 1897): 6.

5. "Aided by Mrs. Pinkham," *Maine Farmer* 66, no. 42 (August 18, 1898): 3.

6. "Mrs. Pinkham Talks about Ovaritis," *Maine Farmer* 66, no. 52 (October 27, 1898).

7. Ibid.

8. "Wise Advice to Husbands," *Maine Farmer* 65, no. 25 (April 22, 1897): 3.

9. Charles H. Pinkham, "Advertising 1875–1953," 1953, 85–86, The Lydia E. Pinkham Medicine Company Records, Schlesinger Library, Radcliffe Institute, Harvard University.

10. Ibid.

11. "Letters, October 13, 1898 to January 19, 1899," The Lydia E. Pinkham Medicine Company Records, Schlesinger Library, Radcliffe Institute, Harvard University quoted in, Engelman, "Face That Haunts Me," 49.

12. Ibid., 49–50; and *Advertisements in Periodicals*, vol. 8, *1924–1929* [advertisements actually go into 1930], The Lydia E. Pinkham Medicine Company Records, Schlesinger Library, Radcliffe Institute, Harvard University.

13. Ibid., 7–8; and Ellen Gruber Garvey, *The Adman in the Parlor: Magazines and the Gendering of Consumer Culture, 1880s to 1910s* (New York: Oxford University Press, 1996), 5, 19–20.

14. Kathy Peiss, *Hope in a Jar: The Making of America's Beauty Culture* (New York: Henry Holt, 1998), 6–8.

15. Engelman, "Face That Haunts Me," 21; and C. H. Pinkham, "Advertising 1875–1953," 1953, 14-15.

16. Engelman, "Face That Haunts Me," 25–26; Lydia E. Pinkham Costal Trading Card, Etsy, https://www.etsy.com/listing/184423794/vintage-1880s-victorian-trade-card-lydia?ref=unav_listing-other; and Lydia E. Pinkham Costal Trading Card, Etsy, https://img1.etsystatic.com/017/0/9235014/il_340x270.578748297_5o57.jpg

17. C. H. Pinkham, "Advertising 1875–1953," 1953, 61–62; and typed sheet with sample trade card of Lydia Pinkham's grandchildren attached, box 93, MC 181, folder 804, The Lydia E. Pinkham Medicine Company Records, Schlesinger Library, Radcliffe Institute, Harvard University.

18. Ibid.

19. Jean Burton, *Lydia Pinkham Is Her Name* (New York: Little and Ives, 1949), 181.

20. Ibid.

21. C. H. Pinkham, "Advertising 1875–1953," 93, appendixes A-12–A-19; and Pinkham pamphlets, MC 181, 2413, "Guide for Women," 7, The Lydia E. Pinkham Medicine Company Records, Schlesinger Library, Radcliffe Institute, Harvard University.

22. Lydia E. Pinkham, *Treatise on the Diseases of Women*, ca. 1901–1908 (EBook 29612), Project Gutenberg, August 5, 2009, chap. 1.

23. Ibid., chap. 4.

24. Ibid., chap. 2.

25. Ibid., chap. 3.

26. Ibid.

27. Ibid., chap. 7.

28. Ibid., chap. 8, fn. 1.

29. Ibid., chaps. 10, 12, and 13.

30. Pinkham pamphlets, MC 181, 2436, no. 104, "War-Time Cook and Health Book," 1918, flyleaf, The Lydia E. Pinkham Medicine Company Records, Schlesinger Library, Radcliffe Institute, Harvard University.

31. Burton, *Lydia Pinkham*, 185; and *Lydia E. Pinkham's Private Text-Book*, passim

32. *Lydia E. Pinkham's Private Text-Book*, 2.

33. Ibid., 5–14.

34. Ibid., 16–22.

35. Ibid., 23–31, 52.

36. Ibid., 50–51.

37. Ibid., 79.

38. C. H. Pinkham, "Advertising 1875–1953," 119.

39. Ibid., 126.

10

Attack of the Muckrakers

An Industry under Siege

Record sales at the close of the nineteenth century had propelled patent medicines to new heights, with a couple thousand companies inundating the market with more than 50,000 products, from potions and lotions to pills that treated ills. But just over the horizon, the winds of change were about to rock the industry and the Lydia Pinkham Company, with both having to defend, in earnest, the medical claims on which their businesses were built.

Up to now, the industry had been able to keep at bay the random critics of its formulas and concoctions. But by the early 1900s, as the Victorian Era continued to give way to the progressive era, a loose coalition of reform-minded journalists, bureaucrats, and health organizations began to raise more questions about food and product safety. In a very short time, patent medicines would be in the crosshairs of an all-out attack designed to shield American consumers from goods identified as healthful without scientific support.[1]

Mark Sullivan and Samuel Hopkins Adams, known in the day as muckrakers for their efforts to root out corruption (real or imagined), wrote a series of articles in the *Ladies' Home Journal* and *Collier's Weekly* that, among other things, raised public awareness about the link between patent medicines and the increasing incidence of drug addiction, both accidental and conscious.[2] Their work and that of others led to the passage of the Pure Food and Drug Act in 1906, a measure that banned interstate traffic of adulterated and misbranded foods and drugs. While the law didn't eradicate the patent medicine industry over night, for many it was the beginning of the end.

In response, some manufacturers had to label whether narcotics, such as opium and cocaine, were part of a product's active ingredients. For the Pinkham Company, the changes meant informing consumers about the compound's specific alcohol content. An inspection program was set up to ensure compliance. Other fraudulent practices were targeted as well, which set up a series of battles with the reformers that would embroil Lydia Pinkham's heirs for decades to come.

Adams immersed himself in research about the patent medicine industry, eventually having the contents of the most popular medicines analyzed by top chemists. He then traveled the country to interview individuals mentioned in testimonial advertisements and people within the industry.[3] Some manufacturers were open and honest, such as Samuel B. Hartman, the German physician who created Peruna, a popular potion used to treat inflammation of the respiratory tract. "I will tell you anything; you can't do us any harm," he told Adams, who wasn't always treated so warmly. Suspicious of him, other owners hired detectives to observe his movements. After he was spotted on a train with a friend's wife, he was told to either stop his investigation or be painted as an adulterer.[4] Ignoring the threats, Adams published the first of ten articles in *Collier's* on October 7, 1905, under the heading "The Great American Fraud." In his introduction, highlighted by the phrase *gullible America*, he noted that

> [America] will spend this year some seventy-five millions of dollars in the purchase of patent medicines. In consideration of this sum it will swallow huge quantities of alcohol, an appalling amount of opiates and narcotics, a wide assortment of varied drugs ranging from powerful and dangerous heart depressants to insidious liver stimulants; and, far in excess of all other ingredients, undiluted fraud.

Adams included a coroner's report and a list of victims who died from the use of patent medicines.[5]

The industry's initial response was subdued, with only two of the 264 medicine companies and individuals who were scrutinized countering with libel suits (that were largely unsuccessful). Later, the response was bolder, as companies pulled their advertising from *Collier's*, with the magazine disclosing that "we spoke out about patent medicines and dropped $80,000 in a year."[6]

Adams then took his protest to Congress, where he engaged in informal lobbying for the Pure Food and Drug bill. Largely on the strength of articles and books by muckrakers of the day, the bill passed, and Adams continued the fight at the state level.[7]

Colleague Sullivan's written salvo, under the heading "The Inside Story of a Sham," exposed the way patent medicine companies obtained testimonial endorsements. He discovered that, although companies almost never paid cash directly to the writers, they did hire a "testimonial broker," who provided letters at a fixed rate. For instance, an endorsement from a U.S. senator would cost seventy-five dollars, while one from a representative would cost forty dollars. Women might lend their names to a testimonial for the cost of a photograph.[8]

In response, and again stretching credibility, the Lydia Pinkham Company asserted, "We never pay for our testimonial letters. Most of our friends are so grateful for the good that they have received by the use of the medicines, that they are glad to tell their friends of it."[9] In truth, some women received cash payments, while others got postage allowances, free medicine, and no-cost photos of themselves. In addition, the company had a few brokers on staff, including one from New York who doubled her profits by selling the same endorsement to a rival.[10]

On another front, ad agent J. T. Wetherald tried to pacify doubters by placing a notice beneath each testimonial promising $5,000 "to any person who will show that the following testimonials are not genuine, or were published before obtaining the writers' special permission."[11] Ostensibly, Wetherald had the proof to back up his claims because the letters came from actual women who wrote to Lydia Pinkham and granted permission to use them in ads. Trouble was that the letters were altered before publication to make them more engaging.[12]

Sullivan and Adams also frequented graveyards in search of testimonial writers who had died. Adams told his readers about a man whose endorsement of Doan's Kidney Pills continued to appear in ads, even though he had died a year earlier of kidney disease.[13]

The reform campaign would continue for years, but even during its height, critics of the Vegetable Compound never claimed that it was especially harmful. Rather, they argued that the product wasn't a particularly effective remedy for any ailment. They also contended that many women relied too heavily on the compound and put off medical treatment until it was too late.

Although the British Medical Association had determined years earlier that the compound "possess[ed] no distinctive characteristics,"[14] one ingredient it did contain in abundance was alcohol. That led muckrakers to compare patent medicines to beer and whiskey, which on the surface was unfortunate timing in that temperance movements, left and right, were demonizing liquor, and the Prohibition era was about to begin a fourteen-year run.[15] The Woman's Christian Temperance Union (WCTU) and others took up the abstinence cause, which hit a snag after magazine editor Edward Bok polled fifty or so members of the WCTU and found that three out of four used patent medicines with alcohol contents of up to 30 percent.[16]

Although the Pinkham Company and its Vegetable Compound generally were able to weather the storm over alcohol, the Pure Food and Drug Act had many other consequences.[17] A common slogan from the reform campaign became "Let the label tell." For the first time, the Vegetable Compound had to list its alcohol content on the label, which read, "18 Per Cent Alcohol" intended "solely as a solvent and preservative." The level was reduced to 15 percent around 1918, but the actual over-the-counter amount was 13.5 percent.[18]

Other label changes ranged from subtle to dramatic. Information that formerly read "A Sure Cure for Prolapsus Uteri" became "For Prolapsus Uteri." The phrase "for all diseases of the kidneys it is the greatest remedy in the world" was eliminated, while "a great help in pregnancy" was changed to "a good help." The claim that the compound could cure "all weaknesses of the generative organs of either sex" also was eliminated. The use of the word *cure* likewise was prohibited (unless there was scientific evidence to prove otherwise). Enforcement of the law was rare, but gradually the word *remedy* replaced *cure*.[19]

The Proprietary Association was a trade group that represented the patent medicine industry, among others.[20] President Frank J. Cheney tried to put the best spin on the circumstances, saying, "It is silly to make me put a new label on my goods just because they have a trifling amount of alcohol in them . . . , but I am willing to put up with the expense, annoyance and trouble this occasions and am not going to kick about it."[21]

Even though patent drug manufacturers had to change their labels, no rules limited access to medicines that might be harmful. The public had to take more responsibility when deciding which products to use. Muckraker Adams once warned, "if you intoxicate yourself with raw alcohol in the form of 'female remedies' or 'catarrh cures,' or play fast and loose with your heart by dosing yourself with headache powders, or drug yourself or your family with morphine or cannabis indica, or chloral, you do so with your eyes open, and the responsibility is upon yourself."[22]

The new law advocated change, but it had limitations. In 1909, Wetherald went back to his old tactics and made bold ad claims, such as when women were quoted saying that the compound had cured their uterine diseases and dissolved tumors. Wetherald also went on the defensive with the compound's critics by addressing their complaints. For example, he placed advertisements that promoted the fact that the alcohol acted merely as a preservative in the compound.[23] He didn't stop there. Fearing that the government might consider classifying the compound an alcoholic beverage, the Pinkham Company contracted with two doctors, who gathered a group of alcoholics and gave them the medicine. Those who sampled the compound said they experienced "no stimulating or exhilarating symptoms" but complained of nausea, headaches, loss of appetite, vomiting, and dizziness. The company rationalized that the symptoms were a reaction to the potency of the herbal ingredients, asserting that its product might even be a cure for alcoholism:

> When nearly through with the bottle, [the subject] began vomiting which persisted all night, could not stand up without falling over; he was more than dizzy, thought his head was whirling around. He had been sick from drink a number of times, but not anywhere near as bad as this. Thought he was going to die, no more of the stuff for him, he was going to cut out all kinds of boozy drinks.[24]

Letters from the company's women customers came under scrutiny, as well. Muckraker journalists, including *Ladies' Home Journal* editor Bok, said that men and women clerks working for patent medicine companies had read and laughed at private letters sent in by female customers. The Pinkham Company claimed that its male employees were prohibited from doing so. Bok also alleged that some clerks would take home the most dramatic letters and share the contents with friends and family for entertainment.[25]

As the attacks mounted, the patent drug industry used its power to influence the press. Because the industry's advertising accounted for one-third of newspaper ad revenue, it could threaten to pull its business if, say, editorials criticizing unfriendly politicians weren't written.[26]

Although generally more cautious about wielding its influence, the Lydia Pinkham Company would do so when pressed. In 1900, two men contracted to hand out pamphlets were arrested and charged with conveying obscene literature under a Pennsylvania law that prohibited the distribution of any material that could be considered obscene. That included information on contraception and other sexual matters.[27] Wetherald arranged for a Wilkes-Barre druggist to secure their release by posting a three-hundred-dollar bond for each. Wetherald then set up a meeting between the town mayor and the two men, who were instructed to remind him of the Pinkham Company's financial impact in the town. The *Philadelphia Inquirer* sent a letter of support, and Wetherald also solicited the help of a former state attorney general living in Wilkes-Barre. The mayor got the charges dropped, and the matter was never made public.[28]

However, the company's encounters with officialdom didn't end there. In 1925, the Food and Drug Administration objected to the wording on Vegetable Compound packaging, saying its cure-all-type claims still promised too much. Production operations were halted until new packaging was printed, and once production was resumed, many employees worked even on Christmas Day to rewrap bottles.[29]

In 1938, in a "scientific opinion" to the Federal Trade Commission, the FDA asserted that the compound was merely a mild stomach tonic that offered no more benefit to women than men. Negotiations over the tentative ruling lasted more than two years before the Pinkham Company signed a stipulation that allowed it to continue with its advertising claim that the compound equated to a uterine sedative.[30]

But the firm's biggest battles were with the American Medical Association (AMA), which among its directives vowed to help keep the nation's drug supply safe by using its influence to discourage sales and the manufacture of "quack or secret medicines."[31] In a compendium of AMA journals, the organization seemed to save its harshest criticisms for the Vegetable Compound, labeling it an ineffective, alcohol-laden fraud. Dr. Arthur Cramp, head of the AMA's Bureau of Investigation, encouraged physicians not to prescribe patent medicines and worked to remove their advertisements from the medical press.[32]

In the mid-1920s, as its influence with consumers grew, the organization focused on convincing the public about the dangers of patent medicines.[33] The effort featured a monthly health magazine launched in 1923 that became a platform to promote its views.[34]

Muckrakers and the AMA differed in their approach to patent medicine advertising. Muckrakers wanted clarity, asking that all ingredients be made known. The AMA felt that the public should not have access to medical advertising because it lacked the proper training.[35] Bok of the *Ladies' Home Journal* quoted a patent medicine maker who asserted,

> Men are "on" to our game: we don't care a damn about them. It is the women we are after. We have buncoed them now for a good many years, and so long as they remain

"easy" as they have been, and we can make them believe that they are sick, we're all right. Give us the women every time. We can make them feel more female troubles in a year than they would really have if they lived to be a hundred.[36]

The constant attacks on the compound and the broader industry eventually took a toll. Although the number of manufacturers grew nearly 30 percent in the decade after the rise of the muckrakers, revenues plateaued and challenges grew.[37] There was a time when the Vegetable Compound received nothing but praise. But as new regulations were enforced and the backlash intensified, consumer sentiment began to sour. Where once there was acclaim and acceptance, there were jokes and sarcasm. Instead of the toast of the town, Lydia became a punchline, in glee club ditties in the early 1880s.[38]

Other songs followed, and some that even took aim at the Pinkham Company's customer base. Eventually, the tide turned again in the 1940s, when Lydia's positive contributions seemed to come back into vogue. That was about the time more big changes came the company's way, changes that in a fashion would mark the end of an era. But that's for another chapter. For now it's time to sing, even if in an unflattering way:

> There's a face that haunts me ever,
> There are eyes mine always meet;
> As I read the morning paper,
> As I walk the crowded street.
> Ah! she knows not how I suffer,
> Her's is now a world-wide fame,
> But, till death, that face shall greet me,
> Lydia Pinkham is her name.[39]

NOTES

1. John Parascandola, "Patent Medicines and the Public's Health," *Public Health Reports* 114, no. 4 (July–August 1999), 318–21.

2. Samuel Hopkins Adams, *Great American Fraud*, (New York: P. F. Collier & Son, 1905, 1906, 1907), 4th ed.

3. Samuel V. Kennedy III, *Samuel Hopkins Adams and the Business of Writing* (Syracuse, NY: Syracuse University Press, 1999), 44.

4. Ibid.

5. Samuel Hopkins Adams, "The Nostrum Evil," *Collier's* (October 7, 1905), reprinted in Samuel Hopkins Adams, *The Great American Fraud* (Chicago: American Medical Association, 1906), 3, 34–35, 47, cited in Sarah Stage, *Female Complaints: Lydia Pinkham and the Business of Women's Medicine* (New York: Norton, 1979).

6. Arthur and Lila Weinberg, *The Muckrakers* (New York: Simon and Schuster, 1961), 176; and Stage, *Female Complaints*, 162–63.

7. Pure Food and Drug Act of 1906, United States Statutes at Large, 59th Cong., sess. I, chap. 3915, pp. 768–72, cited as 34 U.S. Stats. 768 (1906); and Kennedy, *Samuel Hopkins Adams*, 55.

8. Mark Sullivan, "The Inside Story of a Sham," *Ladies' Home Journal* 23, no. 2 (January 1906), 14, cited in Stage, *Female Complaints*.

9. Stage, *Female Complaints*, 165.

10. Ibid.

11. Ibid., 166; and "Joyful Maternity," *Los Angeles Times*, July 5, 1902, 14.

12. Stage, *Female Complaints*, 166.

13. Ibid.

14. Arthur J. Cramp, *Nostrums and Quackery*, vol. 2 (Chicago: Press of American Medical Association, 1921), 161.

15. Samuel Hopkins Adams, "Peruna and the Bracers," *Collier's* (October 28, 1905), reprinted in Samuel Hopkins Adams, *Great American Fraud* (New York: P. F. Collier & Son, 1905, 1906), 16.

16. Edward Bok, "A Few Words to the W.C.T.U.," *Ladies' Home Journal* (September 1904), 16.

17. Stage, *Female Complaints*, 168–70; Mark Sullivan, *Our Times* (New York: Charles Scribner's Sons, 1972), 2:531–50; and Oscar Edward Anderson Jr., *Health of a Nation: Harvey W. Wiley and the Fight for Pure Food* (Chicago: University of Chicago Press, for the University of Cincinnati, 1958), 185–94.

18. Edward J. Julian, "Lydia Pinkham's Legacy," *Boston Sunday Herald Advertiser*, June 16, 1974, "Pictorial Living Magazine" section, 10, in vertical files of the Lynn (MA) Public Library, s.v. Biographies and Obituaries, Pinkham, Lydia; and Stage, *Female Complaints*, 170.

19. Arthur J. Cramp, "Pinkham's Vegetable Compound," *Hygeia* (November 1935): 1013–15; clipping in Pinkham file, Department of Propaganda, American Medical Association, Chicago; and Stage, *Female Complaints*, 170.

20. "About CHPA," *Consumer Healthcare Products Association*, http://www.chpa.org/About.aspx.

21. James Harvey Young, *The Medical Messiahs* (Princeton, NJ: Princeton University Press, 1967), 3–12, 41–65, quoted in James Harvey Young, *American Self-Dosage Medicines: An Historical Perspective* (Lawrence, KS: Coronado, 1974), 16.

22. Samuel Hopkins Adams, "Patent Medicines under the Pure Food Law," *Collier's*, June 8, 1907, reprinted in Adams, *Great American Fraud*, 4th ed., 161, cited in Stage, *Female Complaints*.

23. "Owes Her Life to Lydia E. Pinkham's Vegetable Compound," *Los Angeles Times*, April 8, 1909, section 2, 11; and reading notices, reprinted in Charles H. Pinkham, "Advertising 1875–1953," 1953, 154, The Lydia E. Pinkham Medicine Company Records, Schlesinger Library, Radcliffe Institute, Harvard University, cited in Stage, *Female Complaints*.

24. Stage, *Female Complaints*, 194.

25. Edward Bok, "How the Private Confidences of Women Are Laughed At," *Ladies' Home Journal* (November 1904), reprinted in Adams, *Great American Fraud*, (New York: P. F. Collier & Son, 1905), 95.

26. Peter Conrad and Valerie Leiter, "From Lydia Pinkham to Queen Levitra: Direct-to-Consumer Advertising and Medicalisation," *Sociology of Health and Illness* 30, no. 6 (2008), 827; and Adams, *Great American Fraud*, (New York: P. F. Collier & Son, 1905), 5.

27. Richard J. Evans to the Lydia E. Pinkham Medicine Company, April 4, 1900, box 168, folder 3132, and Lydia E. Pinkham Medicine Company to Richard J. Evans, April 7, 1900,

box 168, folder 3132, both sources found in The Lydia E. Pinkham Medicine Company Records, Schlesinger Library, Radcliffe Institute, Harvard University.

28. Elysa Ream Engelman, "'The Face That Haunts Me Ever': Consumers, Retailers, Critics, and the Branded Personality of Lydia E. Pinkham" (PhD diss., Boston University, 2003), 117; Richard J. Evans to the Lydia E. Pinkham Medicine Company, April 4, 1900, box 168, folder 3132, and Lydia E. Pinkham Medicine Company to Richard J. Evans, April 7, 1900, box 168, folder 3132, both sources found in The Lydia E. Pinkham Medicine Company Records, Schlesinger Library, Radcliffe Institute, Harvard University.

29. Jean Burton, *Lydia Pinkham Is Her Name* (New York: Little and Ives, 1949), 272–73; and Charles H. Pinkham, "Advertising 1875–1953," 1953, 186–87, The Lydia E. Pinkham Medicine Company Records, Schlesinger Library, Radcliffe Institute, Harvard University

30. Burton, *Lydia Pinkham*, 273; and C. H. Pinkham, "Advertising 1875–1953," 209–10 and 214–15.

31. Robert Baker and Linda Emanuel, "The Efficacy of Professional Ethics: The AMA Code of Ethics in Historical and Current Perspective," *Hastings Center Report*, 30, no. 4 (July–August 2000), S14–16.

32. Ibid., S15; Engelman, "Face That Haunts Me," 104; and Cramp, *Nostrums and Quackery*, 160–63.

33. Engelman, "Face That Haunts Me," 137–39; Arthur J. Cramp, "Pinkham's Vegetable Compound," *Hygeia* (November 1935): 1013–15; clipping in Pinkham file, Department of Propaganda, American Medical Association, Chicago; and W. W. Bauer, "Health by Radio Drama," *Hygeia* (October 1935).

34. Ibid., 138–39; W. W. Bauer, "Health by Radio Drama," *Hygeia* (October 1935), 872–73; and "Medicine in the News," *Hygeia* (January 1940), 86.

35. Engelman, "Face That Haunts Me," 106.

36. Edward Bok, "Why 'Patent Medicines' Are Dangerous," *Ladies' Home Journal* 22, no. 4 (March 1905), 18.

37. Engelman, "Face That Haunts Me," 136.

38. "Just a Funny Old Song That Everybody Knows," *True Story* (January 1937), cited in Engelman, "Face That Haunts Me," 156, 159, 267.

39. Burton, *Lydia Pinkham*, 201; Kate Sanborn, "Smith College," *Cincinnati Commercial Tribune*, published as the *Cincinnati Commercial* 42, no. 91, December 25, 1881; "A Picture," quoted in "Pickings and Stealings," *Hamilton Literary Magazine* 16, no. 6 (February 1882), 236; "A Picture," Lydia E. Pinkham, "Lydia's Scrapbook 1870's, 1880's," MC 181, vol. 556, frame 81 of 473 in the author's possession, The Lydia E. Pinkham Medicine Company Records, Schlesinger Library, Radcliffe Institute, Harvard University; Joseph Le Roy Harrison, *Cap and Gown: Some College Verse* (Boston: L. G. Page, 1897), xvi, 161; and "A Picture," *The Cornell Era* 31, no. 4 (October 15, 1898), 47. The origins of this song prove difficult to find. Burton claims the song originated in *The Dartmouth*, where it was found in the December 23, 1881, vol. 3, no. 8, edition. However, it likely came from someone before the publication of the article, and the author is unknown. The clue to this find came from a publication two days later on Christmas Day 1881 in the column by Kate Sanborn, in the *Cincinnati Commercial* of the same verses. Miss Sanborn had strong ties to Dartmouth, where her father, Edwin David Sanborn, was professor and is buried in her family plot in the Dartmouth College Cemetery. Kate Sanborn, English professor at Smith College, in the *Cincinnati Commercial* ended her column on Christmas Day 1881 with the same lines.

11

Times Change, but the Compound Lives On

As America charged into the twentieth century, riding industrialization's wave at the dawn of the auto age, the Lydia Pinkham Company was in midst of a seventy-year run as a force in the world of patent medicines. Before the reign's end in the 1940s, the company would be heralded as a marketing pioneer, and annual product sales would peak at nearly $4 million in 1925. Even later, Lydia would be regarded as one the twenty-five most important women in U.S. history.[1]

But with external and internal pressures building almost daily, a long period of modification and retrenchment was about to sweep over the Pinkhams and the Goves, leaving their venerable brand bruised and its reputation battered. As safety and reform measures for the entire industry took hold at the national level, the Vegetable Compound and its rivals had to be reformulated, setting off a chain reaction of aftereffects with far-reaching consequences. Since before the Civil War, patent medicines had been pitched as miracle cures for almost any ailment. But now those claims had to be tempered, and for some manufacturers their dangerous mix of cocaine, opium, and alcohol had to be minimized or discontinued.

For the Pinkham Company, the new directives meant making the first in a series of changes to a formula and label that had gone untouched for nearly forty years. In essence, federal mandates in 1914 said the Vegetable Compound was not medicated enough to keep it from being classified as a beverage, which would make it subject to a higher tax rate. To gain compliance, dandelion, yellow gentian, and the base of bitter Swiss cordial were added, while the alcohol content was reduced from 18 percent to 15 percent, yielding a thicker solution.[2] Sales and profits initially held their own, but the formula change would lead to a host of problems, seemingly without end.[3]

Manufacturing issues surfaced when the lower amounts of alcohol proved insufficient to suspend the higher amounts of botanical matter, allowing a thick sediment to form at the bottom of the medicine bottle. Fermentation soured the compound's taste, prompting druggists to return shipments, and other sediment issues ensued that required enormous amounts of attention.[4] Label changes only aggravated the situation because the company had to back off or discontinue claims that federal agencies now deemed false and misleading.

For decades, compound labels read,

A Sure Cure for Prolapsus Uteri or falling of the Womb, and all female weaknesses, including Leucorrhea, Painful Menstruation, Inflamation and Ulceration of the Womb, Irregularities, Floodings, etc. Pleasant to the taste, efficacious and immediate in its effect. It is a great help in pregnancy, and relieves pain during labor. For All Weaknesses of the generative organs of either Sex, it is second to no remedy that has ever been before the public; and for all diseases of the Kidneys it is the Greatest Remedy in the World.

The modified label read, "Recommended for the treatment of non-surgical cases of Weakness and Disorders of the Female Generative Organs. Pleasant to the taste and strongly recommended as efficacious and as a good help in pregnancy and for relieving pain during labor."[5]

Not only did this lessen the compound's appeal with consumers, but also within five years, the company in advertisements was laying bare its manufacturing process for all to see.[6] Before long, revenue struggled to keep pace with rising taxes, manufacturing costs, and overhead. To compensate, in the roaring years before the Great Depression, the company threw more and more money into its advertising, a move that eventually would break the twenty-year peace between the Pinkhams and Goves.

Initially, agent J. T. Wetherald increased advertising 9 percent, which boosted sales 16 percent. Even though subsequent increases produced poorer results and worries about the effectiveness of key strategies, he kept on spending on newspaper ads as big as sixty inches (ten inches on six columns) that were tied to testimonials.[7] Years later, in a spurt of creativity inspired by famous ad man J. Stirling Getchell, a piece from 1931 featured a woman telling her husband, "I'm sorry . . . not tonight!" Although the straitlaced Pinkhams were not amused, response to the ad helped the company show a $400,000 profit for the year after recording a loss of $260,000 the previous year.[8]

Pamphlets also would continue to be a part of the Pinkham Company arsenal because they could be distributed quickly, efficiently, and inexpensively.[9] In questionnaires inserted in 1920, 98 out of every 100 respondents said the compound benefited them in some way, giving rise in later newspaper ads to the phrase "98 Out of 100 Women Benefited."[10]

Ad spending often generated debate in the Pinkham Company boardroom. By the mid-1920s, Arthur Pinkham had become president after Will Gove's death, and Aroline had passed her treasurer's spot to daughter Lydia Pinkham Gove. Lydia Gove, who stood quite tall at 6'2", never had much patience for new advertising strategies, always preferring to spend about 50 percent of ad sales on testimonials. Arthur, along with his brothers, vice president Daniel and secretary Charles Jr., favored diversification and didn't think expenditures should exceed more than 30 percent of sales. This was one of many areas of dispute between the two families. Legend had it that, before Charles Pinkham died in 1900, he sent sister Aroline a letter suggesting that his wife succeed him as president upon his death. However, it was Aroline's husband, Will Gove, who gained control of the company. Disagreements continued, and on one occasion, Lydia Gove locked company securities in a safe deposit box and ran away with the key. As assistant treasurer, she often skipped out on meetings where votes required unanimous support for passage. Daniel, speaking on the subject of Lydia Gove, said she was determined to "run the business or ruin it."[11]

The feud went on hiatus in 1926, when Lydia Gove became the first woman to fly on a cross-country flight. With the accomplishment and in a letter to *Editor and Publisher*, Lydia Pinkham Gove generated a fair amount of publicity for the company and the compound:

Lynn, Mass., Sept. 17, 1926

First let me introduce myself. I am Lydia Pinkham Gove, granddaughter of Lydia E. Pinkham, assistant treasurer of the Lydia E. Pinkham Medicine Company, and actively engaged in the management of the business in the capacity of advertising manager and purchasing agent. While traveling with my brothers, Mrs. William Pinkham Gove, and her three children, the idea occurred to me and the conductor of our little party, Rev. James Luther Adams, assistant pastor of the Second Unitarian Church in Salem, to fly from Los Angeles, Cal., to Portland, Me., and land in Boston. Both Mr. Adams and I had enjoyed so much our flights from Los Angeles to San Diego, Riverside and Santa Barbara, that we decided immediately to cross the continent by airplane, and the next day we were on our way, leaving the rest of the party to proceed homeward by train.[12]

Although Lydia Gove, 40, tried to distance herself from any talk of a publicity stunt by saying the flight was about making history not about advertising for her "grandmother's famous Vegetable Compound," the company cashed in on the public's interest. A *Pinkham Pioneers* pamphlet recounted every phase of the flight on parts of pages and used the other halves for product testimonials.[13]

The family bickering quickly resumed against the backdrop of the Great Depression, and control of the company was at stake by early 1935, when almost $1.5 million was spent on advertising, which represented 80 percent of sales. The mounting losses played into Lydia Gove's hands because her plan was to drive the company toward insolvency in hopes she could buy the Pinkhams' stock and gain control. As treasurer, she had unilaterally taken on loans she refused to pay off, which prompted Charles Jr. to stop turning money over to her. Lydia Gove blocked advertising expenditures for six months, which in 1936 pushed the two sides into court for five tumultuous years. In July 1937, the Pinkham men were granted a permanent injunction against the Gove women that prevented them from interfering in the business. The long legal battle, in which a countersuit was dismissed in 1941, crippled the company for a time and sent Lydia Gove into reclusion.[14]

A new round of clashes with federal agencies, this time pitting the company against President Franklin D. Roosevelt's New Deal administration, were up next but not before a few moral victories in the court of public opinion set the families' heirs up for one last big deal.

By this time, the company had at least moved out of the AMA's doghouse, with the organization saying claims and ingredients were more properly lined up.[15] In 1941, compound ads featured such less-bold phrases as "Distress from Monthly Female Weakness, Woman's 'Trying-Years' 38–52 Years Old, Relieves Monthly Female Pain, Female Periodic Complaints, Monthly Pain, Dysmenorrhea." Gone were promises of dissolving tumors and curing kidney troubles. The shift accompanied a new promotional emphasis on the company's pills, driven by the fact the government was levying a heavier tax on alcohol, which cut into profits and meant compound production could not be increased.[16] The first radio spots also were added to the mix in 1940, followed later by one-minute movie trailers.[17]

But no matter the platform, the company's message was being muted by advancements in other areas of medicine that threatened to make the compound obsolete. Competition from vaccines, hormone therapies, and antibiotics not only were revolutionizing the pharmaceutical industry but also making botanical remedies afterthoughts.[18]

In one last burst of glory, however, the Vegetable Compound figuratively got off the mat after being sucker punched by the Federal Trade Commission in 1938. As part of New Deal protocols, the agency threatened to block any claims that the product was an "adequate treatment for any female condition." Follow-up research on the compound paid for by the company found that not only was it effective in reducing hot flashes in women but also was helpful in easing menstrual pain by establishing a "normal rhythm in a previously arrhythmic contractile pattern, and to eliminate superimposed contractions on the normal contractile phase."[19] Researchers said compound users experienced a type of estrogen therapy almost 100 years before that type of treatment was even given a name.[20] Later analysis, in mid-1949, determined the estrogenic properties also were found in the Vegetable Compound.[21]

Although significant for the Pinkhams, the victory was a hollow one on many levels. By the 1950s, the company and Lydia's image were both showing their age. To younger consumers, her portrait wasn't that of a lovable grandmother; it was a liability, and an old one to boot. As advertising trends and modern-day rivals not only caught up with the company but also surpassed it, there was no way diminishing sales could keep the firm alive.

Before he died in 1960 at age eighty-one, Arthur must have watched in pain as the company languished through lean years. A ghost of its former self, the Lydia E. Pinkham Company was swallowed up in 1968 by Cooper Laboratories, a global pharmaceutical company based in California that paid $1 million dollars for its aging customer base and fading brand. Cooper moved the plant operations from Lynn to Puerto Rico to be closer to raw materials and cheap labor. In 1979, the compound was said to gross $700,000 in sales, while in 1981 more than 150,000 bottles were sold, according to spokesman Del Marks of Cooper.[22]

Cooper Laboratories sold the brand to pharmaceutical giant Johnson & Johnson, which held onto it briefly before turning it and three other brands over to Numark Laboratories in 1987.[23] The latter is run by Bob Stites, Moaiz Daya, Ben Deavenport, Pat Lonergan, and Lou Sullivan, who left Johnson & Johnson to start Numark, based in New Jersey. Sales of the compound on the Internet and by word of mouth have increased moderately the past few years, nearing $1 million annually, according to Numark's public relations department.[24] The compound is available through eBay, Amazon, HealthCareExpress.com, and Pharmacy Rx by the sixteen-ounce bottle for fourteen to sixteen dollars and in tablet form for nine to twelve dollars per seventy-two-count box. Directions tell users to take a single tablespoon three times a day with meals, adding that mixing the compound with fruit juice is OK. In the remedy's heyday, the Pinkham Company directed the user to take "one tablespoonful every four hours," presumably to go through the mixture faster.[25] Present-day ingredients are

> Water, Fructose, Ascorbic Acid (Vitamin C), Dogwood Bark, Motherwart Leaf, Flavor, Dandelion Root, Alcohol 10%, Pleurisy Root, Licorice Root, Salicylic Acid, Edetic Acid, Sodium Benzoate, Black Cohosh Root, Dl-Alpha Tocopheryl Acetate (Vitamin E), BHA, Butylparaben, Gentian Root.[26]

Numark Labs added motherwort, an herb from the mint family, in 1992 as a substance "to alleviate the symptoms of menopause."[27] Note, too, that the alcohol content has been reduced even further, down to 10 percent, roughly the same as a bottle of Nyquil.[28]

Although alcohol is used today as a solvent and preservative, it seems appropriate to put it to more traditional use with a toast to the Pinkhams and Goves, despite their teetotal ways. Although testimonial advertising for the compound is a thing of the past, some consumers still write to Numark, full of praise for the product. In 2002, an 80-year-old woman said the formula helped relieve stress, while a 55-year-old woman recently wrote that four generations of her family have used the remedy for symptoms related to menstruation and mild depression.[29] Here's to some customs, nurtured through triumph and tragedy, that will never die.

NOTES

1. "The 25 Most Important Women in American History," *Ladies' Home Journal* (July 1986), 85, 127; and Cecil Munsey, "Lydia's Medicine, 130 Years Later," 2003, http://cecilmunsey.com/index.php?option=com_docman&task=doc_download&gid=788&&Itemid=34.

2. Charles H. Pinkham, "Advertising 1875–1953," 1953, 150, The Lydia E. Pinkham Medicine Company Records, Schlesinger Library, Radcliffe Institute, Harvard University; and Jean Burton, *Lydia Pinkham Is Her Name* (New York: Little and Ives, 1949), 271.

3. C. H. Pinkham, "Advertising 1875–1953," 150.

4. Ibid.

5. Ibid.

6. [No title], *The Salt Lake Telegram* (Salt Lake City, UT), September 22, 1919.

7. C. H. Pinkham, "Advertising 1875–1953," 160.

8. John McDonough and Karen Egolf, eds., "J. Stirling Getchell, Inc.," *The Advertising Age Encyclopedia of Advertising*, vol. 2, *F–O* (New York: Fitzroy Dearborn, 2003), 669.

9. C. H. Pinkham, "Advertising 1875–1953," 169.

10. Ibid., 172.

11. "Family Trouble," *Time* 27, no. 18 (May 4, 1936), 74, *Academic Search Premier*; and "Lydia Loses," *Time* 37, no. 9 (March 3, 1941): 71–73, *Academic Search Premier*.

12. Lydia Pinkham Gove, letter to the editor, "The Pinkham Flight," *Editor and Publisher* (September 25, 1926), 65; and "Pinkham Puts over Big Publicity Stunt," *Editor and Publisher* (September 11, 1926), 45.

13. Burton, *Lydia Pinkham*, 255, 257; and *Pinkham Pioneers*, booklet 137 in C. H. Pinkham, "Advertising 1875–1953," A-17.

14. C. H. Pinkham, "Advertising 1875–1953," 196–97; and Munsey, "Lydia's Medicine."

15. "Lydia Pinkham's New Dress," *Time* 33, no. 1 (January 2, 1939), 18; and Sarah Stage, *Female Complaints: Lydia Pinkham and the Business of Women's Medicine* (New York: Norton), 243.

16. C. H. Pinkham, "Advertising 1875–1953," 261–62.

17. Ibid., 265.

18. "Pharmaceutical Industry," *Encyclopaedia Britannica Online Academic Edition*, 2014, http://www.britannica.com/EBchecked/topic/1357082/pharmaceutical-industry.

19. Burton, *Lydia Pinkham*, 273–74.

20. Ibid., 275–77.

21. Ibid., 276–77.

22. "Arthur Pinkham of Medicine Firm: Grandson of Founder Dies—Won 40-Year Court Fight for Company Control," *New York Times*, January 1, 1961, 48; "Ask the Globe," *Boston Globe*, March 14, 1982; and Munsey, "Lydia's Medicine."

23. Public Relations Office, Numark Labs, Edison, NJ, in discussion with the author, April 10, 2011; and Moaiz Daya (vice president, Numark Labs), in discussion with the author, 2012.

24. Moaiz Daya and Bob Stites, e-mail correspondence with the author, November 13–14, 2013; "Company Profile," *Numark Laboratories*, http://www.numarklabs.com/index.php?src=gendocs&ref=CompanyProfile; and "Biographies," *Numark Laboraties*, http://www.numarklabs.com/index.php?src=gendocs&ref=Biographies.

25. "Lydia Pinkham Herbal Liquid Supplement," *HealthCareExpress.com*, http://www.healthcareexpress.com/cf/Lydia_Pinkham_Herbal_Liquid_Supplemen-147.html?ItemNum=129&search=all&setback=1=Nutritional%20Supplements; and Munsey, "Lydia's Medicine," figure 16.

26. "Lydia Pinkham Herbal Liquid Supplement"; Lydia Pinkham Herbal Liquid Supplement, box, Supplement Facts, Numark Laboratories, Edison, New Jersey, 2012.

27. Dorry Baird Norris, *Lydia Pinkham: Herbal Entrepreneur* (Franklin, TN: Sage Cottage, 1996), 13.

28. Munsey, "Lydia's Medicine"; and "Vicks Nyquil Cold and Flu Nighttime Relief," http://dailymed.nlm.nih.gov/dailymed/archives/fdaDrugInfo.cfm?archiveid=57766.

12

Call Her Good, Call Her Bad, Call Her a Success

Woman business pioneer or disgraced national nightmare? Suffragette healer or tee-total hypocrite? Single-minded savior or double-dealing huckster? History has, and will continue to, judge Lydia Pinkham, but no matter the moral verdicts, she was by most accounts a good mother, solid citizen, and savvy entrepreneur. Perhaps that last title is the best one to measure her by because she stepped up and took risks at a time when most women were content to stay in the background, out of the way, away from the fray.

Lydia was always different, championing equal-rights causes at an early age at a time when the divide between men and women was deep and between blacks and whites was even deeper. Who knows what drove her to see wrongs and try to right them, to spot suffering and try to heal it, and to encounter injustice and try to conquer it. She challenged convention, authority, and bureaucracy with nothing more than belief in herself, her family, and her home remedies. Lydia Pinkham was not only ahead of her time but also helped define the times in which she lived.[1] Well after she was gone, her contributions were remembered by small-town newspapers and national publications alike. Taking her place alongside the likes of civil rights icon Rosa Parks, First Lady Martha Washington, and astronaut Sally Ride, she has been regarded in some circles as one of the most important women in U.S. history.[2]

But in an especially confounding paradox, this is the same woman who many argue slipped alcohol to the unknowing for financial gain, preyed on women's fears for the sake of self-aggrandizement, and built an empire based on "The Great American Fraud."[3]

In publicizing one series of muckraking stories in the early 1900s about Lydia and her patent medicine ilk, *Collier's* magazine said,

> These articles . . . will not only describe the methods used to humbug the public into buying patent medicines through fake testimonials and lying statements published in the newspapers, but will show that a large number of the so-called "tonics" are only cocktails in disguise, and that many of these [remedies] are directly responsible for the making of drunkards and drug fiends.[4]

Other critics reserved for her such labels as profiteer, scammer, and cheat.

Perhaps such attacks came with the territory because Lydia and her company were taking on powerful institutions and cutting into the profits of equally powerful industrialists of the day. But make no mistake, there were plenty of villains to go around in what then passed for the business of health care, from those shilling "cure-all" potions to those "practicing medicine" by using leeches to do their dirty work on unsuspecting women wracked with menstrual pain. Even though those were simpler times, there was little innocent about the late 1800s if you were a victim of either of those treatments.

Lydia Pinkham probably was a saint and a sinner, not unlike other heroines of yesterday and today. She not only put together a company that at one time employed about 450 people but also came up with a product that hit the shelves in 1875 and that today is still doing a million-dollars' worth of business annually. The Vegetable Compound, on which the Pinkhams spent more than $200 million (adjusted for 2014 inflation) to promote over the course of a century, also helped them turn a profit in all but a handful of those years.[5] The family's effective use of mass advertising in newspapers, magazines, and trading cards marked the emergence of modern-day direct-to-consumer pharmaceutical marketing. Not bad for a product that by most accounts was a powerfully tasting potion.

But suppose, as some critics charge, the alcohol-laden Vegetable Compound was effective only in convincing women to put off needed medical treatment until it was too late for them to be helped? Let's say the countless women who wrote testimonials to Lydia did so in blind faith of an elixir that actually sped their demise? What if, in the colorful yet sordid history of patent medicines, there were no good guys but only bad ones painted in shades of gray? That may help us put Lydia in her historical place, but it might not do justice to the woman whose face launched a thousand ads.

Whichever side of the debate you favor, consider that although hindsight often offers the most accurate view of history, it doesn't always provide one that is true.

NOTES

1. "The Greatest Women," *Patriot* (Harrisburg, PA), vol. 68, no. 300 (January 8, 1912), 6.
2. "The 25 Most Important Women in American History," *Ladies' Home Journal* (July 1986), 85, 127.

3. Samuel Hopkins Adams, "The Nostrum Evil," *Collier's* (October 7, 1905), reprinted in Samuel Hopkins Adams, *The Great American Fraud* (Chicago: American Medical Association, 1906), 3–5.

4. *Collier's* (September 30, 1905), quoted in Arthur Weinberg and Lila Weinberg, *The Muckrakers* (New York: Simon and Schuster, 1961), 177.

5. Cecil Munsey, "Lydia's Medicine, 130 Years Later," 2003, http://cecilmunsey.com/index.php?option=com_docman&task=doc_download&gid=788&&Itemid=34; and "Inflation Calculator," *Dave Manuel.com*, http://www.davemanuel.com/inflation-calculator.php.

Bibliography

BOOKS

Adams, Samuel Hopkins. *The Great American Fraud*. Chicago: American Medical Association, 1906.

Anderson, Ann. *Snake Oil, Hustlers, and Hambones: The American Medicine Show*. Jefferson, NC: McFarland, 2000.

Anderson, Oscar Edward, Jr. *Health of a Nation: Harvey W. Wiley and the Fight for Pure Food*. Chicago: University of Chicago Press, for the University of Cincinnati, 1958.

Atherton, Lewis. *Main Street on the Middle Border*. Bloomington: Indiana University Press, 1954.

Austin, George Lowell. *Perils of American Women*. Boston: Lee and Shepard, 1883.

Beecher, Catharine E. *Letters to the People on Health and Happiness*. New York: Harper, 1855.

Bennet, James Henry. *Inflammation of the Uterus*. 3rd ed. London: John Churchill, 1853.

Bowker, Richard R. *Copyright, Its History and Its Law*. Boston: Houghton Mifflin, 1912.

Brown, John A. *The Family Guide to Health*. Providence, RI: B. T. Albro, 1837. Digitized by Open Knowledge Commons, U.S. National Library of Medicine.

Burchard, Peter. *Frederick Douglass for the Great Family of Man*. New York: Atheneum Books for Young Readers, 2003.

Burton, Jean. *Lydia Pinkham Is Her Name*. New York: Little and Ives, 1949.

Clark, Thomas D. *Southern Country Editor*. Indianapolis: Bobbs-Merrill, 1948.

Clutterbuck, Henry. *Proper Administration of Blood-Letting for the Prevention and Cure of Disease*. London: S. Highley, 1840.

Collier, Robert. "The Secret of the Ages." (Originally published: New York: Robert Collier, 1926), (Global Grey edition, E-Book, 2013), 198.

Commander, Lydia Kingsmill. *The American Idea*. New York: Barnes, 1907.

Cramp, Arthur J. *Nostrums and Quackery*. Vol. 2. Chicago: American Medical Association, 1921.

———. *Nostrums and Quackery*. Vol. 3. Chicago: American Medical Association, 1936.

Dawley, Alan. *Class and Community: The Industrial Revolution in Lynn.* Cambridge, MA: Harvard University Press, 1976.

Dickey, Marcus. *The Youth of James Whitcomb Riley.* Indianapolis: Bobbs-Merrill, 1919.

Douglass, Frederick. *Life and Times of Frederick Douglass.* Boston: De Wolfe, Fiske, 1893.

——. *My Bondage and My Freedom.* New York: Miller, Orton and Mulligan, 1855.

——. *Narrative of the Life of Frederick Douglass, an American Slave.* 1845. Reprint, Cambridge, MA: Belknap Press of Harvard University Press, 1988.

Estes, Charles. *Estes Genealogies 1097–1893.* Salem, MA: Eben Putnam, 1894.

Faulkner, Carol. *Women's Radical Reconstruction: The Freedmen's Aid Movement.* Philadelphia: University of Pennsylvania Press, 2004.

Garvey, Ellen Gruber. *The Adman in the Parlor: Magazines and the Gendering of Consumer Culture, 1880s to 1910s.* New York: Oxford University Press, 1996.

Gilman, Charlotte Perkins. *Women and Economics.* Boston: Small, Maynard, 1898.

Harrison, Joseph La Roy. *Cap and Gown: Some College Verse.* Boston: L. G. Page, 1897.

Hartley, Florence. *The Ladies' Book of Etiquette and Manual of Politeness.* Boston: Lee & Shepard, Publishers, 1872.

Henry, O. "Jeff Peters as a Personal Magnet." In *The Gentle Grafter* (18–32). Garden City, NY: Doubleday, Page, 1908.

Hollick, Frederick. *The Origin of Life and the Process of Reproduction.* New York: American News, 1878.

Holmes, Oliver Wendell. *Medical Essays 1842–1882.* Cambridge, MA: Riverside Press, Houghton, Mifflin, 1892.

Hubbard, Elbert. *Lydia E. Pinkham: Being a Sketch of Her Life and Times.* East Aurora, NY: Roycrofters, 1915.

Hudson, Wade. *Powerful Words.* New York: Scholastic, 2004.

Hutchinson, John Wallace. *Story of the Hutchinsons: Tribe of Jesse.* Boston: Lee and Shepard, 1896.

Jameson, Edwin M. *Gynecology and Obstetrics.* New York: Hoeber, 1936.

Kennedy, Samuel V., III. *Samuel Hopkins Adams and the Business of Writing.* Syracuse, NY: Syracuse University Press, 1999.

King, John. *The American Dispensatory.* 8th ed. Cincinnati: Wilstach, Baldwin, 1870.

——. *The American Dispensatory.* 10th ed. Cincinnati: Wilstach, Baldwin, 1876.

Knowlton, Charles. *Fruits of Philosophy: An Essay on the Population Question.* 2nd new ed. London: Free Thought, 1877.

Kwolek-Folland, Angel. *Incorporating Women: A History of Women and Business in the United States.* New York: Twayne, 1998.

Lewis, Alonzo, and James R. Newhall. *History of Lynn, Essex County Massachusetts, Including Lynnfield, Saugus, Swampscot, and Nahant.* Boston: John L. Shorey, 1865.

Link, Eugene Perry. *The Social Ideas of American Physicians.* London: Associated University Presses, 1992.

Livermore, Mary A. Introductory letter to *Perils of American Women,* by George Lowell Austin. Boston: Lee and Shepard, 1883.

Marshall, W. G. *Through America.* London: Sampson Low, Marston, Searle, and Rivington, 1881.

McDonough, John, and Karen Egolf, eds. *The Advertising Age Encyclopedia of Advertising.* New York: Fitzroy Dearborn, 2003.

McFeely, William S. *Frederick Douglass.* New York: W. W. Norton, 1991.

McNamara, Brooks. *Step Right Up*. Garden City, NY: Doubleday, 1976.

Meigs, Charles D. *Females and Their Diseases*. Philadelphia: Lea and Blanchard, 1848.

Michelet, Jules. *L'Amour*. New York: Carleton, 1868. Translated from the 4th Paris edition by J. W. Palmer.

Mitchell, Sally. *Daily Life in Victorian England*. Westport, CT: Greenwood Press, 1996.

Moses, Wilson Jeremiah. *Creative Conflict in African American Thought*. New York: Cambridge University Press, 2004.

Norris, Dorry Baird. *Lydia Pinkham: Herbal Entrepreneur*. Franklin, TN: Sage Cottage, 1996.

Pancoast, Charles L. *Trail Blazers of Advertising*. New York: Grafton Press, 1926.

Peiss, Kathy. *Hope in a Jar: The Making of America's Beauty Culture*. New York: Henry Holt, 1998.

Pinkham, Lydia E. *Lydia E. Pinkham's Private Text-Book upon Ailments Peculiar to Women*. Lynn, MA: Lydia Pinkham Medicine Co., 1905.

———. *Treatise on the Diseases of Women*. 1901 & 1904. EBook 29612, Project Gutenberg, August 5, 2009.

Rogers, William B. *We Are All Together Now*. New York: Garland, 1995.

Rothstein, William G. *American Physicians in the Nineteenth Century*. Baltimore: Johns Hopkins Press, 1972.

Rush, Benjamin. *Six Introductory Lectures, to Courses of Lectures, upon the Institutes and Practices of Medicine, Delivered in the University of Pennsylvania*. Philadelphia: Conrad, 1801.

Rutkow, Ira. *Seeking the Cure*. New York: Scribner, 2010.

Shryock, Richard Harrison. *Medicine and Society in America, 1660–1860*. New York: University Press, 1960.

Stage, Sarah. *Female Complaints: Lydia Pinkham and the Business of Women's Medicine*. New York: Norton, 1979.

Starr, Paul. *The Social Transformation of American Medicine*. New York: Basic Books, 1982.

Sullivan, Mark. *Our Times*. New York: Charles Scribner's Sons, 1972.

Theriot, Nancy M. *Mothers and Daughters in Nineteenth-Century America*. Lexington, KY: The University Press of Kentucky, 1996.

Thomson, John. *A Vindication of the Thomsonian System*. Albany, NY: Webster and Wood, 1825.

Thomson, Samuel. *Narrative of the Life and Medical Discoveries of Samuel Thomson*. 5th ed. St. Clairsville, OH: Horton Howard, 1829.

———. *New Guide to Health*. 2nd ed. Boston: J. Q. Adams, 1835.

Twitchell, James B. *Twenty Ads That Shook the World: The Century's Most Groundbreaking Advertising and How It Changed Us All*. New York: Three Rivers, 2000.

Veblen, Thorstein. *The Theory of the Leisure Class*. Oxford: Oxford University Press, 2007. First published 1899 by Macmillan.

Venning, Frank D. *Wildflowers of North America: A Guide to Field Identification*. New York: St. Martin's, 2001.

Walsh, Mary R. *"Doctors Wanted, No Women Need Apply": Sexual Barries in the Medical Profession, 1835–1975*. New Haven, CT: Yale University Press, 1978.

Washburn, Robert Collyer. *The Life and Times of Lydia Pinkham*. New York: G. P. Putnam's Sons, 1931.

Webber, Malcom. *Medicine Show*. Caldwell, ID: Caxton Printers, 1941.

Weeks, Joseph D. "Reports on the Manufacture of Glass." In *Report of the Manufactures of the United States at the Tenth Census*. Washington, DC, 1883.

Weinberg, Arthur, and Lila Weinberg. *The Muckrakers*. New York: Simon and Schuster, 1961.

Wesley, John. *Primitive Physic.* Originally published in 1747, London: J. Paramore. Revised by William M. Cornell, Boston: Cyrus Stone, 1858.

Woodhouse, Barbara Bennett. *Hidden in Plain Sight.* Princeton, NJ: Princeton University Press, 2008.

Young, James Harvey. *American Self-Dosage Medicines: An Historical Perspective.* Lawrence, KS: Coronado, 1974.

———. *The Medical Messiahs.* Princeton, NJ: Princeton University Press, 1967.

———. *The Toadstool Millionaires: A Social History of Patent Medicines in America before Federal Regulation.* Princeton, NJ: Princeton University Press, 1961.

DISSERTATIONS

Engelman, Elysa Ream. "'The Face That Haunts Me Ever': Consumers, Retailers, Critics, and the Branded Personality of Lydia E. Pinkham." PhD diss., Boston University, 2003.

Faler, Paul Gustaf. "Workingmen, Mechanics and Social Change: Lynn, Massachusetts 1800–1860." PhD diss., University of Wisconsin, 1971.

MANUSCRIPTS

"Advertisements in Periodicals, vol. 1, 1890–1900." The Lydia E. Pinkham Medicine Company Records, Schlesinger Library, Radcliffe Institute, Harvard University.

"Advertisements in Periodicals, vol. 2, 1901–1902." Lydia E. Pinkham Medicine Company, The Lydia E. Pinkham Medicine Company Records, Schlesinger Library, Radcliffe Institute, Harvard University.

"Advertisements in Periodicals, vol. 7, 1920–1923." Lydia E. Pinkham Medicine Company, The Lydia E. Pinkham Medicine Company Records, Schlesinger Library, Radcliffe Institute, Harvard University.

"Advertisements in Periodicals, vol. 8, 1924–1929." [Advertisements actually go into 1930.] The Lydia E. Pinkham Medicine Company Records, Schlesinger Library, Radcliffe Institute, Harvard University.

Bigelow, Jacob. "On Self Limited Diseases." Paper presented before the Massachusetts Medical Society, May 27, 1835. Reprinted in *Medical America in the Nineteenth Century: Readings from the Literature*, edited by Gert H. Brieger. Baltimore: Johns Hopkins Press, 1972.

Cross, C. F. Letters to Charles H. Pinkham, March 4, 1881, and March 15, 1881. Box 167, folder 3125. The Lydia E. Pinkham Medicine Company Records, Schlesinger Library, Radcliffe Institute, Harvard University.

Evans, Richard J. Letter to the Lydia E. Pinkham Medicine Company, April 4, 1900. Box 168, folder 3132. The Lydia E. Pinkham Medicine Company Records, Schlesinger Library, Radcliffe Institute, Harvard University.

Gove, William H. Letter to Charles H. Pinkham, October 17, 1884. Box 168, folder 3133a. The Lydia E. Pinkham Medicine Company Records, Schlesinger Library, Radcliffe Institute, Harvard University.

Helfand, William H. "Historical Images of the Drug Market-XXXVII," *Pharmacy in History. American Institute of the History of Pharmacy*, 1991, vol. 35, no. 1.

Hubbard, H. P. "The Story of *Lydia Pinkham*." *Fame* (November 1892). Typescript, MC 181, 3035. The Lydia E. Pinkham Medicine Company Records, Schlesinger Library, Radcliffe Institute, Harvard University.

Lydia E. Pinkham Medicine Company. Letter to Richard J. Evans, April 7, 1900. Box 168, folder 3132. The Lydia E. Pinkham Medicine Company Records, Schlesinger Library, Radcliffe Institute, Harvard University.

"The Lydia E. Pinkham Plant, History of Mfg. Process." MC 181 2635. The Lydia E. Pinkham Medicine Company Records, Schlesinger Library, Radcliffe Institute, Harvard University.

"Making a Medicine." N.d. MC 181, 2635. The Lydia E. Pinkham Medicine Company Records, Schlesinger Library, Radcliffe Institute, Harvard University.

"Partnership Agreement." October 18, 1881. Box 164, folder 3043. The Lydia E. Pinkham Medicine Company Records, Schlesinger Library, Radcliffe Institute, Harvard University.

"A Picture." In "Lydia's Scrapbook 1870's, 1880's," by Lydia E. Pinkham. MC 181, vol. 556. The Lydia E. Pinkham Medicine Company Records, Schlesinger Library, Radcliffe Institute, Harvard University.

Pinkham, Charles H. "Advertising 1875–1953." 1953. Box 93, MC 181, folder 804. The Lydia E. Pinkham Medicine Company Records, Schlesinger Library, Radcliffe Institute, Harvard University.

Pinkham, Charles H., and H. P. Hubbard. Agreement, December 27, 1883. Box 84, folder 763. The Lydia E. Pinkham Medicine Company Records, Schlesinger Library, Radcliffe Institute, Harvard University.

Pinkham, Daniel, and Guy N. F. Ford. Correspondence, April 19, 1938, December 7, 1939, and January 11, 1940. Box 168, folder 3156. The Lydia E. Pinkham Medicine Company Records, Schlesinger Library, Radcliffe Institute, Harvard University.

Pinkham, Daniel R. Letters to William Pinkham, 1876–1879. Typescripts, box 181, folder 3118. The Lydia E. Pinkham Medicine Company Records, Schlesinger Library, Radcliffe Institute, Harvard University.

Pinkham, Lydia. "Journal of Lydia E. Pinkham." Box 180, folder 3365. The Lydia E. Pinkham Medicine Company Records, Schlesinger Library, Radcliffe Institute, Harvard University.

———. "Medical Directions for Ailments," vol. 537. Ca. 1878. The Lydia E. Pinkham Medicine Company Records, Schlesinger Library, Radcliffe Institute, Harvard University.

———. Minutes of the Freemans Institute, January 19, 1843. "Notebook of Lydia E. Pinkham, Including Minutes of Freemans Institute, 1848–1865." The Lydia E. Pinkham Medicine Company Records, Schlesinger Library, Radcliffe Institute, Harvard University.

"Politics and Rum." Ca. November 1879. In "Lydia's Scrapbook, 1870's, 1880's," by Lydia E. Pinkham. MC 181, vol. 556.

"Process of Manufacture." N.d. MC 181, 2635. The Lydia E. Pinkham Medicine Company Records, Schlesinger Library, Radcliffe Institute, Harvard University.

Reading notices. Reprinted in *Advertising*, vol. 328, by Charles Pinkham, 154. The Lydia E. Pinkham Medicine Company Records, Schlesinger Library, Radcliffe Institute, Harvard University.

Riznik, Barnes. "Medicine in New England, 1790–1840." Unpublished manuscript, 1963. Old Sturbridge Village, MA.

"Stock Certificates." Box 164, folder 3047. The Lydia E. Pinkham Medicine Company Records, Schlesinger Library, Radcliffe Institute, Harvard University.

Wright, Henry G. "Vegetable Diet." Lecture and discussion at the Freemans Institute, Lynn, MA, January 24, 1843. Recorded in minutes of the Freemans Institute. In "Notebook of Lydia E. Pinkham, Including Minutes of Freemans Institute, 1848–1865," by Lydia Pinkham. Folder 3365. The Lydia E. Pinkham Medicine Company Records, Schlesinger Library, Radcliffe Institute, Harvard University.

PAMPHLETS

"Guide for Women." 1893, Pinkham pamphlets. MC 181, 2413. The Lydia E. Pinkham Medicine Company Records, Schlesinger Library, Radcliffe Institute, Harvard University.

"Help for Women." 1910. Pinkham Pamphlets. MC 181, 2427, no. 66. The Lydia E. Pinkham Medicine Company Records, Schlesinger Library, Radcliffe Institute, Harvard University.

"How We Visited the Laboratory." 1908. In "The Lydia E. Pinkham Plant, History of Mfg. Process." MC 181, 2635. The Lydia E. Pinkham Medicine Company Records, Schlesinger Library, Radcliffe Institute, Harvard University.

"Pinkham Pioneers." Lynn, MA: Lydia E. Pinkham Medicine Company, 1927. MC 181, 2456, booklet 137. The Lydia E. Pinkham Medicine Company Records, Schlesinger Library, Radcliffe Institute, Harvard University.

"War-Time Cook and Health Book." 1918. Pinkham pamphlets, MC 181, 2436, no.104. The Lydia E. Pinkham Medicine Company Records, Schlesinger Library, Radcliffe Institute, Harvard University.

"Women's Letters." 1914. Pinkham pamphlets, MC 181, 2431, Mail distribution. The Lydia E. Pinkham Medicine Company Records, Schlesinger Library, Radcliffe Institute, Harvard University.

PERIODICALS AND REPORTS

"The 25 Most Important Women in American History." *Ladies' Home Journal.* July 1986.

"Abuses of Proprietary Remedies." *Pharmaceutical Era.* February 28, 1895.

"Aided by Mrs. Pinkham." *Maine Farmer,* vol. 66, no. 42. August 18, 1898.

American Nonconformist (Indianapolis), no. 740. August 30, 1894.

Anaconda Standard (Anaconda, MT) 12, no. 139. January 27, 1901.

Baker, Robert, and Linda Emanuel. "The Efficacy of Professional Ethics: The AMA Code of Ethics in Historical and Current Perspective." *Hastings Center Report* 30, no. 4. July–August 2000.

Bauer, W. W. "Health by Radio Drama." *Hygeia.* October 1935.

Bell, Whitfield J., Jr. "Suggestions for Research in the Local History of Medicine in the United States." *Bulletin of the History of Medicine* 17 (1945).

Berkshire County Whig (Pittsfield, MA), vol. 6, no. 265. April 4, 1846.

Bok, Edward. "A Few Words to the W.C.T.U." *Ladies' Home Journal.* September 1904.

———. "Why 'Patent Medicines' Are Dangerous." *Ladies Home Journal.* vol. 22, no. 4, March 1905.

Boston Herald. June 6, 1890.

Boston Herald. "I am not well enough to work," July 8, 1890.

Boston Herald. "If We Only Had Children!," May 25, 1890.

Burt, Elizabeth V. "From 'True Woman' to 'New Woman.'" *Journalism History* 37, no. 4 (Winter 2012).

"The Come and See Sign." *Michigan Farmer*, vol. 53, no. 17. April 25, 1908.

Conrad, Peter, and Valerie Leiter. "From Lydia Pinkham to Queen Levitra: Direct-to-Consumer Advertising and Medicalisation." *Sociology of Health and Illness* 30, no. 6 (2008).

Cooper, E. R. "Check on Counterfeit Goods." *Pharmaceutical Era.* June 14, 1900.

Cornell Era, "A Picture." vol. 31, no. 4. October 15, 1898.

Cramp, Arthur J. "Pinkham's Vegetable Compound." *Hygeia* (November 1935).

"Cutters Who Continue to Cut." *Pharmaceutical Era.* January 30, 1896,

Daily Evening Item. (Lynn, MA), "Lydia Pinkham Dead." May 18, 1883.

———. "Only Sour Beer." December 21, 1883.

Dartmouth, "A Picture." vol. 3, no. 8. December 23, 1881.

"The Department Store." *Pharmaceutical Era.* May 30, 1895.

"Department Store Fight." *Pharmaceutical Era.* April 4, 1895.

"The Department Store Octopus." *Pharmaceutical Era.* May 23, 1895.

Douglass, Frederick. "Letter from Frederick Douglass." *Boston Daily Advertiser*, no. 108. November 4, 1859.

———. "Miscellany: Letter from Frederick Douglass." *Barre Patriot* (Barre, MA), vol. 2, no. 33. March 3, 1846.

———. "To Capt. Thomas Alud, Formerly My Master." *Liberator* (Boston), no. 37. September 14, 1849.

Druggist Circular, no. 49 (1905): 30.

Edstrom, David. "Medicine Man of the '80s." *Reader's Digest*, no. 32. June 1938.

"Family Trouble." *Time*, vol. 27, no. 18. May 4, 1936.

Georgian (Savannah, GA), "Vegetable Tooth Powder," vol. 5, no. 66. February 12, 1824.

Gove, Lydia Pinkham. "The Pinkham Flight." Letter to the editor. *Editor and Publisher.* September 25, 1926.

"Greenback Meeting and Convention." *The Farmers' Cabinet* (Amherst, NH), vol. 77, no. 10. November 10, 1878.

Inter Ocean [published as *The Daily Inter Ocean* (Chicago)], "Intellectual Habit: Petition of an Employee in a Certain Medicine Company," vol. 22, no. 287. January 7, 1894.

Julian, Edward J. "Lydia Pinkham's Legacy." *Boston Sunday Herald Advertiser* section 10 (June 16, 1974) [Pictorial Living Magazine]. In vertical files of the Lynn (MA) Public Library, s.v., Biographies and Obituaries, Pinkham, Lydia.

"Just a Funny Old Song That Everybody Knows." *True Story* 35, no. 6. January 1937.

Kansas City Times (Kansas City, MO). February 6, 1885.

Kimball, Arthur P. "The Age of Disfigurement." *Outlook*, no. 57, October 30, 1897.

Liberator quoted in the *Herald of Freedom*, "Clerical Impudence—The Climax." September 2, 1842.

Liberator (Boston), no. 24, June 14, 1844.

"A Life's Experience." *Lippincott's Monthly Magazine.* November 1892.

Los Angeles Times. "Joyful Maternity." July 5, 1902.

———. "Owes Her Life to Lydia E. Pinkham's Vegetable Compound." April 8, 1909.

"Lydia Loses." *Time*, vol. 37, no. 9. March 3, 1941.

"Lydia E. Pinkham's Vegetable Compound Is a Positive Cure." *Michigan Farmer.* June 12, 1883.

"Lydia Pinkham's New Dress." *Time*, vol. 33, no. 1. January 2, 1939.

Macon Telegraph [published as the *Telegraph and Messenger* (Macon, GA)], "Lydia Pinkham." no. 10373. May 20, 1883.

"A Medicine for a Woman. Invented by a Woman. Prepared by a Woman." *Youth's Companion*, vol. 55, no. 41. October 12, 1882.

"Medicine in the News." *Hygeia* (January 1940).

Morning Chronicle (New York), no. 723. "Dr. Cooley's Vegetable Elixir." February 8, 1805.

Moulton, Roy K. "Moulton Lead from the Editor's Pencil." *Kalamazoo Gazette* (Kalamazoo, MI). March 4, 1914.

"Mrs. Pinkham Talks about Ovaritis." *Maine Farmer*, vol. 66, no. 52. October 27, 1898.

New Haven Register (New Haven, CT), vol. 42, no. 52. "Persons and Things." March 3, 1882.

New Haven Register [published as the *New Haven Evening Register* (New Haven, CT)], vol. 61, no. 119. "Lydia Pinkham; Paralysis." May 19, 1883.

New York Herald. "Lincoln Ad." February 26, 1861.

New York Times. "Arthur Pinkham of Medicine Firm: Grandson of Founder Dies—Won 40-Year Court Fight for Company Control." January 1, 1961.

———. "Voted for Lydia Pinkham." November 23, 1934.

New-York Tribune "An Intolerable Nuisance." May 13, 1876.

North American (Philadelphia, PA), "I am a Living Witness of the Wonderful and Miraculous Effects of Lydia E. Pinkham's Vegetable Compound," April 2, 1896.

N.Y. Mercury. "Turlington's Original Balsam of Life." November 9, 1761.

O'Brien, C. C. "'The White Women All Go for Sex': Frances Harper on Suffrage, Citizenship, and the Reconstruction South." *African American Review* 43, no. 4 (Winter 2009).

Olch, Peter. "William S. Halsted and Local Anesthesia: Contributions and Complications." *Anesthesiology* 42 (1975).

Oregonian [published as the *Sunday Oregonian* (Portland, OR)]. "Our Sisters, Our Cousins, and Our Aunts." June 29, 1883.

Parascandola, John. "Patent Medicines and the Public's Health." *Public Health Reports* 114, no. 4 (July–August 1999).

Patriot (Harrisburg, PA), "The Greatest Women." vol. 68, no. 300. January 8, 1912.

"Pickings and Stealings." *Hamilton Literary Magazine*, vol. 16, no. 6. February 1882.

"Pinkham Puts over Big Publicity Stunt." *Editor and Publisher*. September 11, 1926.

Plain Dealer (Cleveland, OH), vol. 39, no. 28. "News in Brief." February 1, 1883.

Portsmouth Oracle, "Roger's Vegetable Pulmonic Detergent." vol. 22, no. 30. April 27, 1811.

Salt Lake Telegram (Salt Lake City, UT). September 22, 1919.

Sanborn, Kate. "Smith College." *Cincinnati Commercial Tribune* [published as the *Cincinnati Commercial*], vol. 42, no. 91. December 25, 1881.

"The Sin of Substitution." *Pharmaceutical Era*, vol. 13, no. 14. March 21, 1895.

Smith-Rosenberg, Carroll, and Charles Rosenberg. "The Female Animal: Medical and Biological Views of Woman and Her Role in Nineteenth-Century America." *Journal of American History* 60, no. 2 (September 1973).

"Speech of Frederick Douglass, Recently Delivered at a Large Temperance Meeting in London." *Journal of the American Temperance Union* 9, no. 1 (January 1845).

Stern, Earle. "Old Recipe Made Lydia Pinkham Household Word." *Item* (Lynn, MA), December 24, 1968.

Sullivan, Mark. "The Inside Story of a Sham." *Ladies' Home Journal*, vol. 23, no. 2. January 1906.

Sunday Herald (Boston). May 28, 1899.

Sunday Times-Herald. "Death of Lydia E. Pinkham's Son; Popular Head of Great Business." November 11, 1900.

Texas Siftings (Austin, TX), vol. 3, no. 7. June 23, 1883.

Themis (Sacramento, CA), vol. 4, no. 39. "Book Chat." November 12, 1892.

"These Cutters Discouraged." *Pharmaceutical Era.* May 2, 1895.

Times-Picayune (New Orleans, LA). November 2, 1882.

———. April 15, 1883.

———. [published as the *Daily Picayune* (New Orleans, LA)]. "Lydia Pinkham." June 24, 1883.

Trenton Evening Times [published as the *Trenton Times* (Trenton, NJ)]. "Lydia Pinkham; Brooklyn Bridge." May 23, 1883.

———. "Mrs. Lydia Pinkham." May 21, 1883.

"Tribute to a Mother Interview with Charles H. Pinkham: Malicious Stories about Lydia E. Pinkham." *Ohio Farmer (1856—1906),* vol. 89, no. 20. May 14, 1896.

Trieger, Bob. "Lydia Pinkham Sold an Image." *Daily Item* (Lynn, MA). April 6, 1999.

Tyler, Varro E. "Was Lydia E. Pinkham's Vegetable Compound an Effective Remedy?" *Pharmacy in History* 37, no. 1 (1995).

"Wise Advice to Husbands." *Maine Farmer,* vol. 65, no. 25. April 22, 1897.

"Wise Advice to Husbands." *Massachusetts Ploughman and New England Journal of Agriculture* 56, no. 27 (April 3, 1897).

Yaeger, Dan. "The Lady Who Helped Ladies." *Yankee* 53, no. 9. September 1989.

Young, James Harvey. "Arthur Cramp: Quackery Foe," *Pharmacy in History,* American Institute of the History of Pharmacy, vol. 37, no. 4, (1995).

———. "Folk into Fake." Special issue, "Healing, Magic, and Religion," *Western Folklore* 44, no. 3 (July 1985).

WEBSITES

Copies of all the websites have been retained by the author, lest the websites becomes inactive.

"(1888) Frederick Douglass on Woman Suffrage." *BlackPast.org* http://www.blackpast.org/1888-frederick-douglass-woman-suffrage.

"About CHPA." *Consumer Healthcare Products Association.* http://www.chpa.org/About.aspx.

Ancestry.com, Massachusetts, Death Records, 1841–1915 [online database] (Provo, UT: Ancestry.com Operations, 2013). Original data: *Massachusetts Vital Records, 1840–1911* (Boston: New England Historic Genealogical Society); and *Massachusetts Vital Records, 1911–1915* (Boston: New England Historic Genealogical Society). http://search.ancestry.com/search/db.aspx?dbid=2101.

Ancestry.com, Massachusetts, Marriage Records, 1840–1915 [online database] (Provo, UT: Ancestry.com Operations, 2013). Original Data: *Massachusetts Vital Records, 1840–1911* (Boston: New England Historic Genealogical Society); and *Massachusetts Vital Records, 1911–1915* (Boston: New England Historic Genealogical Society). http://search.ancestry.com/search/db.aspx?dbid=2511.

Ancestry.com, Massachusetts, Town and Vital Records, 1620–1988 [online database] (Provo, UT: Ancestry.com Operations, 2011). Original data: Town and City Clerks of Massachusetts,

Massachusetts Vital and Town Records (Provo, UT: Holbrook Research Institute, Jay and Delene Holbrook). http://search.ancestry.com/search/db.aspx?dbid=2495.

Ancestry.com, Vermont, Vital Records, 1720–1908 [online database] (Provo, UT: Ancestry.com Operations, 2013). Original data: State of Vermont, *Vermont Vital Records through 1870* (Boston: New England Historic Genealogical Society); and State of Vermont, *Vermont Vital Records, 1871–1908* (Boston: New England Historic Genealogical Society). http://search.ancestry.com/search/db.aspx?dbid=4661.

Bachelder, J. B. "Lynn Massachusetts detailed birds-eye view." *Album of New England Scenery* (1856). http://www.skinnerinc.com/auctions/2494/lots/615.

"Biographies." *Numark Laboraties.* http://www.numarklabs.com/index.php?src=gendocs&ref =Biographies.

"Births Registered in the City of Lynn, for the Year 1852." *Massachusetts Vital Records, 1841–1915.* Microfilm no. 1,420,835, Family History Library, Salt Lake City, UT. https://familysearch.org/pal:/MM9.3.1/TH-266-12876-20082-87?cc=1536925.

"Blood, How Much Do We Have?" *MedicineNet.com.* http://www.medicinenet.com/script/main/art.asp?articlekey=21474.

"Bloodletting Is Back! Here's Everything You Need to Know about This Ancient Practice." *Medtech.* http://www.medtech.edu/blog/the-history-progression-and-modern-stance-on-bloodletting.

Bruno, Gwen. "Why Was There Bloodletting in Barber Shops?" *eHow.* http://www.ehow.com/facts_5719000_there-bloodletting-barber-shops_.html.

Bulletin for the History of Chemistry 28, no. 1 (2003). http://www.scs.illinois.edu/~mainzv/HIST/bulletin_open_access/v28-1/v28-1%20p9-17.pdf.

"Chromolithograph." Boston Public Library, Print Department. http://en.wikipedia.org/wiki/File:Lydia_E._Pinkhams_cures_and_claims.jpg.

"The Coming of Drink to New England (1620–1820)." *Maine Historical Society.* http://www.mainehistory.org/rum-riot-reform/1620-1820/index.html.

"Creating the Ether Dome Painting." *Massachusetts General Hospital.* http://www.massgeneral.org/history/exhibits/ether-dome-painting.

"Elizabeth Blackwell." *Bio.* http://www.biography.com/people/elizabeth-blackwell-9214198.

"Estes." *Ancestry.com.* http://freepages.genealogy.rootsweb.ancestry.com/~fdmoore/estes.htm.

"Ether and Chloroform," *History.com,* http://www.history.com/topics/ether-and-chloroform.

"Ether inhaler, ca. 1840's." *Countway Repository.* http://repository.countway.harvard.edu/xmlui/handle/10473/1785.

Find A Grave. http://www.findagrave.com.

Finley, Harry. *Patent Medicine Etc.: Lydia Pinkham.* http://www.mum.org/mrspin17.htm.

"Fruit and Vegetable Compound Offers Hope against Gum Disease." *HealthCanal.* October 18, 2011. http://www.healthcanal.com/oral-dental-health/22004-Fruit-and-vegetable-compound-offers-hope-against-gum-disease.html.

"Greenback Party." *The Free Dictionary.* http://www.thefreedictionary.com/Greenback+Party.

Higby, Gregory J. "Chemistry and the 19th-Century American Pharmacist." *Bulletin for the History of Chemistry,* Volume 28, Number 1 (2003), http://www.scs.illinois.edu/~mainzv/HIST/bulletin_open_access/v28-1/v28-1%20p9-17.pdf.

"Hippocrates Quotes." *Goodreads.* http://www.goodreads.com/author/quotes/248774.Hippocrates.

"History of Patent Medicine." *Hagley Museum and Library.* http://www.hagley.org/online_exhibits/patentmed/history/history.html.

Hoffman, Robert B., and Donald E. Martin. "The History of Modern Anesthesia." *Pennsylvania Society of Anesthesiologists*. http://www.psanes.org/Home/tabid/37/anid/43/Default.aspx.

Huff, Ethan A. "Vegetable Compound May Prevent, Treat Arthritis." *Natural News*. September 16, 2010. http://www.naturalnews.com/029757_sulforaphane_arthritis.html.

"Inflation Calculator." *Dave Manuel.com*. http://www.davemanuel.com/inflation-calculator.php.

"Literature Trail: Alonzo Lewis and Lynn Writers." *Escapes North*. http://www.escapesnorth.com/trail_lit/trail.php?sec=&trail=23.

"Lydia Pinkham Herbal Liquid Supplement." *HealthCareExpress.com*. http://www.healthcare-express.com/cf/Lydia_Pinkham_Herbal_Liquid_Supplemen-147.html?ItemNum=129&search=all&setback=1=Nutritional%20Supplements.

"Mary Baker Eddy: Life." *Mary Baker Eddy Library*. http://www.marybakereddylibrary.org/mary-baker-eddy/life.

"Massachusetts, Births and Christenings, 1639-1915," index, *FamilySearch* https://familysearch.org/pal:/MM9.1.1/VQXG-BFC, FHL microfilm 0397791 V. 1. https://familysearch.org/pal:/MM9.1.1/VQXG-2QL, FHL microfilm 0397791 V. 1. https://familysearch.org/pal:/MM9.1.1/VQXG-2Q5, FHL microfilm 0397791 V. 1. https://familysearch.org/pal:/MM9.1.1/VQXG-P3T, FHL microfilm 0397791 V. 1. https://familysearch.org/pal:/MM9.1.1/V5NC-TKJ, FHL microfilms 0547549, 0878650, 0877737, 0877738, 877736.

"Massachusetts, Births, 1841-1915," index and images, *FamilySearch*. https://familysearch.org/pal:/MM9.1.1/FXCW-G86, FHL microfilm 1420835.

"Massachusetts, Deaths and Burials, 1795-1910," index, *FamilySearch*. https://familysearch.org/pal:/MM9.1.1/FH6L-F31, FHL microfilm 1927788.

"Massachusetts, Deaths, 1841-1915," index and images, *FamilySearch*. https://familysearch.org/pal:/MM9.1.1/NWCL-336, FHL microfilm 959810. https://familysearch.org/pal:/MM9.1.1/NW2H-KJK, FHL microfilm 960220. https://familysearch.org/pal:/MM9.1.1/NW2H-LMJ, FHL microfilm 960220. https://familysearch.org/pal:/MM9.1.1/N7GD-V24, FHL microfilm 960224. https://familysearch.org/pal:/MM9.1.1/NWCR-BKX, FHL microfilm 960240. https://familysearch.org/pal:/MM9.1.1/N7JR-F2P, FHL microfilm 1420527. https://familysearch.org/pal:/MM9.1.1/NW61-J46, FHL microfilm 959806. https://familysearch.org/pal:/MM9.1.1/N7JR-FP2, FHL microfilm 1420527. https://familysearch.org/pal:/MM9.1.1/NW61-J2Z, FHL microfilm 959806. https://familysearch.org/pal:/MM9.1.1/N7T2-JFN, FHL microfilm 960222.

"Massachusetts, Marriages, 1841–1915," index and images, *FamilySearch*. https://familysearch.org/pal:/MM9.1.1/NW5J-QJ2, FHL microfilm 1432995.

Munsey, Cecil. "Lydia's Medicine, 130 Years Later." *CecilMunsey.com*. 2003. http://cecilmunsey.com/index.php?option=com_docman&task=doc_download&gid=788&&Itemid=34.

"The Panic of 1873." *History Engine*. http://historyengine.richmond.edu/episodes/view/308.

"Patent Medicine." *Dictonary.com*. http://dictionary.reference.com/browse/patent+medicine.

"Patients' Voices in Early 19th Century Virginia." *University of Virginia*. http://carmichael.lib.virginia.edu/story/tools.html.

"Pharmaceutical Industry." *Encyclopaedia Britannica*. http://www.britannica.com/EBchecked/topic/1357082/pharmaceutical-industry.

"The Remarkable Lydia Pinkham." *In-Gender.com*. www.in-gender.com/gender-selection/lydia-pinkham/LydiaPinkham_Story.aspx.

"Rosa Parks Biography." *Academy of Achievement*. http://www.achievement.org/autodoc/page/par0bio-1.

Schmid, Jennifer. "Beautiful Black Poison." *The Weston A. Price Foundation*. 2009. http://www.westonaprice.org/.

"Vegetable-Based Drug Could Inhibit Melanoma." *Phys.org*. March 1, 2009. http://phys.org/news155132202.html.

"Vegetable Compounds Effective in Treating Triple-Negative Breast Cancer, Study Shows." *Huffington Post*. October 17, 2012. http://www.huffingtonpost.com/2012/10/17/vegetable-compounds-effective-triple- negative-breast-cancer_n_1975343.html.

"Vermont, Vital Records, 1760–1954," index and images, *FamilySearch*. https://familysearch.org/pal:/MM9.1.1/XFJL-M68, FHL microfilm 27542. https://familysearch.org/pal:/MM9.1.1/V8ML-SHD, FHL microfilm 27657.

"Vicks Nyquil Cold and Flu Nighttime Relief." *DailyMed*. http://dailymed.nlm.nih.gov/dailymed/archives/fdaDrugInfo.cfm?archiveid=57766.

"Victoria (r. 1837–1901)." *The Official Website of the British Monarchy*. http://www.royal.gov.uk/historyofthemonarchy/kingsandqueensoftheunitedkingdom/thehanoverians/victoria.aspx.

"Was Columbus Greek," *Greece Travel.com*. http://www.greecetravel.com/history/columbus/.

Waring, Belle. "Commodification Meets Black Cohosh," NLM Seminar Focuses on 19th-Century Patent Medicine (April 7, 2006). http://nihrecord.od.nih.gov/newsletters/2006/04_07_2006/story04.htm.

MISCELLANEOUS

B., Gordon. *Lydia E. Pinkham*, original painting in Schlesinger Library, Radcliffe Institute, Harvard University.

Ciuli, Ettore. "Storia generale dell' esplorazione." Illustration in *Nuove Dimostrazioni di Ostetricia*, by J. P. (Jacques Pierre) Maygrier. Pisa: Nistri, 1831.

Daya, Moaiz, Numark vice president, conversation with the author, 2012.

Daya, Moaiz and Bob Stites, e-mail correspondence to the author, November 13-14, 2013.

Keva, Bette. Pine Grove Cemetery. Hackmatack Avenue, Lot 1343, Grave 8, Lydia, Lynn, MA, 2012.

Murphy, Jessica B. Center for the History of Medicine Francis A. Countway Library of Medicine, Harvard Medical School, phone and email conversations with the author." Public Relations Office, Numark Labs, Edison, NJ, telephone conversation between company spokesman and the author, April 10, 2011.

Pure Food and Drug Act. United States Statutes at Large. 59th Cong., sess. 1, chap. 3915, p. 768–72. 1906.

"Supplement Facts." On Lydia Pinkham Herbal Liquid Supplement Box. Numark Laboratories, Edison, NJ, 2012.

Index

About the Author

Sammy R. Danna, PhD, before his retirement in 2012, was a full professor of communication at Loyola University Chicago for more than thirty years. He taught at the school from 1969 to 2012. Among his courses were public speaking and critical thinking, radio and television production, introduction to advertising and advanced advertising, mass communication law, and history of advertising and public relations. He is the author of more than ninety articles, book chapters, and monographs. Two of the chapters are in an enduring book, *Advertising and Popular Culture*, which he also edited.

He has delivered more than forty papers and chaired almost as many sessions at Popular Culture Association (PCA) conventions nationally and internationally since 1980 and has chaired the PCA Advertising Area since 1986. Dr. Danna, who earned the rank of professor emeritus at Loyola, received his PhD in communication from the University of Missouri–Columbia. He also holds three master's degrees: in speech education, secondary/higher education, and theology. While completing this Lydia Pinkham volume, he began work on a book about the unsung soda fountain's remarkable but little-known impact on American history.